BRIGHT iDEAS

Art

D1422156

Written by Mary Lack

Published by Scholastic Ltd, Villiers House,
Clarendon Ave, Leamington Spa,
Warwickshire CV32 5PR

© 1991 Mary Lack
10 11 12 13 14 15   7 8 9 0

Written by Mary Lack
Edited by Janet Fisher
Sub-edited by Christine Lee
Illustrated by Mary Lack
Front and back covers: designed by Sue Limb,
photographs by Martyn Chillmaid, work by
Mary Lack
Artwork by Liz Preece, Castle Graphics,
Kenilworth

Printed in Great Britain by Ebenezer Baylis,
Worcester

**British Library Cataloguing in Publication
Data**
Lack, Mary
    Bright ideas – arts.
    1. Primary schools. Curriculum subjects. Visual arts
    I. Title
    707.1

    ISBN 0-590-76559-0

Contents

4 INTRODUCTION

6 BASIC SKILLS
Drawing basic shapes   7
Patterns with lines   8
Looking at texture   9
Tissue paper collage   9
Building it up   10
Self-portraits   11
Drawing still life   14
Giant food models   16

18 BASIC TECHNIQUES
Resist painting   19
Marbled beads   20
Plaster casts   20
Cut paper patterns   21
Monoprint greetings
    cards   22
Thumb pot   23
Stick pot   24
Painted beads   25
Printing shapes   26
Butterflying   27
Stencilled cards   28
Positive/negative images   29

String-printed art folder   30
Tie-dyed fabric   31
Moulded clay dish   33
Paper folding   33
Paper weaving   34
Design a tile   34
Felt picture   35
Marbled paper   37
Tessellations 1   38
Tessellations 2   39
Freestanding plaster form   40
Plastering scrap   41

42 MAKING PICTURES
Fish tank   43
A dragon collage   44
Circus frieze   45
Rock pool collage   46
A printed fruit bowl   47
Easter eggs   47
A painted landscape   48
A favourite toy   49

50 MATERIALS
Pebble pictures   51
Printing with packaging   52

Bottle mobiles 52
Decorative hangings 53
Cotton reel sculptures 54
Making a screen 55
Bottle fish 56
A woven hanging 57
Wristbands 58
A fleecy wall-hanging 59
Camouflage nets 60

62 NATURAL OBJECTS

Leaf drawings 63
Collage of leaf rubbings 64
Marbled jewellery 65
Painted jewellery 66
Feather designs 67
Shell designs 69
Sunflower plaque 70
Felt jewellery 71
String collage 72
Leaf dish in clay 73
Fruit embroidery 74

76 PATTERNS

Crayon resist pattern 77
Stained glass windows 78
Mosaic patterns 79
A triangle card 80
A printed card 81
Using triangles 82
A felt bag 83

84 GEOMETRIC SHAPES

Sponge printing 85
Over-printing with
  sponge 86
Geometric jewellery 86
Cardboard jewellery 87
Geometric relief 88
Cardboard box sculpture 89
Dyed string collage 90
Hanging sculpture 90
Papier-mâché cone 91

Tiled panels 92
Balloon mould vessels 93

94 COLOUR AND LIGHT

Colour sorting 95
Rainbow picture 96
Colour mixing 97
Paper collage 98
Woven panel 99
Stained glass roundels 100
Experiments with colour 101
Night light holder 102
Card sculpture 103
Make a mobile 107

108 GLOSSARY

110 REPRODUCIBLE MATERIAL

126 RESOURCES

Introduction

Why should art be part of the school curriculum, and what is meant by the term 'art', anyway?

Perhaps if we replace 'art' with 'visual communication', the relevance of the activities grouped under that umbrella term will become more obvious.

Normally, we tend to think of any communication as being verbal. However, words are just one form of communication. We also communicate in other ways, for instance, through music which has its own language. Music communicates through the language of sound, using the grammar of rhythm, melody, volume, harmony, discord and so on.

Similarly, 'art', or 'visual communication', has its own language. To be visually literate, we need to have an understanding of, among other things, colour, light, shape, form and proportion. These comprise a basic visual grammar which is relevant not only to painting and sculpture, but also to architecture, graphics (the most obvious form of visual communication), furniture, interiors, textiles, industrial design, ceramics and television.

The United Kingdom has a long tradition of providing superb visual education through art colleges and polytechnics, but we must ensure that children don't have to wait until their tertiary education before they are encouraged to appreciate visual designs. To get the message across and start the ball rolling early, politicians, business people, teachers and parents all have to understand and appreciate the importance of visual design.

CAN ART BE TAUGHT?

It is generally accepted that skills in verbal languages, or subjects such as music and mathematics can be taught. Art, however, is popularly supposed to be 'a gift' – either you're born with it or you're not. This is a misconception.

Just as in any other discipline, the basic language can be taught and learned. Obviously, some pupils will show more aptitude than others, but this is true in any subject. Just as ability in music or mathematics has to be developed, so does ability in visual skills.

For the non-specialist teacher this can be a great worry. Many feel insecure and inadequate through lack of understanding and training; others enjoy visual work but feel too pressured to consider teaching yet another subject in a new way.

This book aims to support the non-specialist teacher, and those under stress, by providing activities which will help to develop children's visual literacy.

ABOUT THIS BOOK

This book comprises eight chapters. The first two, Basic skills and Basic techniques, include activities which introduce skills such as drawing and modelling and make use of a wide range of materials and techniques. The subsequent chapters include activities which are based on specific subjects or areas, such as colour and natural objects.

Most of the activities use basic materials which are easy to obtain and, while suggestions are made for finished products, there is still considerable scope for developing children's creativity.

Basic skills

Teaching children to observe and record are the main aims of the activities in this chapter. The easiest ones are concerned with looking at, and differentiating between, lines, basic shapes, colours and textures, and then recording and commenting on them in a simple way.

When the children have grasped these skills, they will be able to tackle more complex subjects, such as natural objects, in which the elements previously considered individually, are combined.

Drawing a self-portrait and still life are even more complex, but there are suggestions for tackling them logically, such as breaking them down into basic shapes, which have helped many beginners.

Drawing basic shapes

Age range
Five upwards.

Group size
Individuals.

What you need
A variety of paper shapes (for example, squares, circles and triangles) or copies of photocopiable pages 111 and 112, paper, crayons.

What to do
With the whole class, look at the shapes and make sure that the children recognise them. Rotate the shapes as in Figure 1, and ask the children if they can still identify them. Then ask the children to draw the shapes using crayons. Draw examples for them to copy if necessary or allow them to use the templates on photocopiable pages 111 and 112.

Next, talk about the shapes, and ask the children which objects look similar to them. For example, a square might represent a house, while two circles could resemble a bird or small animal, provided that extra details such as windows and doors for the house and ears, eyes and paws for the animal were added. Then let the children draw some more shapes and turn them into pictures.

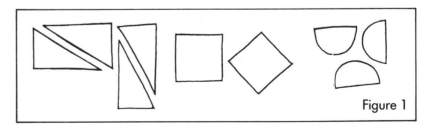

Figure 1

Patterns with lines

Age range
Five upwards.

Group size
Individuals.

What you need
Paper, drawing tools (such as crayons, felt-tipped pens).

What to do
Draw various patterns on the chalkboard using curved and straight lines. Talk to the children about each pattern as you draw it, discussing features such as whether a line is curved or straight.

When the children can differentiate between the two, go on to talk about more complex lines, such as zig-zags, and lines which have straight and curved parts. This discussion session need not last long, but it should help children to look at lines and patterns more closely.

Afterwards, encourage the children to draw their own patterns, filling a sheet of paper with combinations of the examples you have drawn on the board (plus any they can think of themselves). Let them fill in the patterns with coloured felt-tipped pens or crayons.

Looking at texture

Age range
Five upwards.

Group size
Individuals or whole class.

What you need
Scrap materials, including fabric, wood shavings, string, sandpaper and other materials with distinct textures, sugar paper, adhesive, scissors.

What to do
As a class, look at and feel each type of material in turn, discussing its texture and surface qualities. Use words like soft, smooth, fluffy, hard, gritty, knobbly and so on. Then invite the children to stick pieces of the materials on to the sugar paper, arranging them in an attractive pattern.

Tissue paper collage

Age range
Six upwards.

Group size
Individuals.

What you need
White paper, tissue paper in a variety of colours, adhesive, spreaders, scissors (optional).

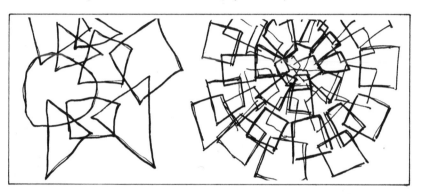

What to do
Cut the tissue paper into fairly small pieces in advance to avoid waste.

Look at the colours with the children and make sure that they recognise them. Show them how different colours can be overlapped to make more colours.

Encourage the children to make collages using torn or cut tissue paper. Show them how to apply adhesive to the background, and smooth the paper on to it. Remind them to overlap colours. The designs could be abstract, or perhaps based on a stained glass window, with colours radiating from a central point, and changing like a rainbow.

Building it up

Age range
Seven upwards.

Group size
Individuals.

What you need
A building (viewed through a window if necessary), paper, drawing materials.

What to do
With the children, look carefully at the chosen building. To help them to look for the relevant information, ask them questions. The first thing to look at is proportion, so they need to look at heights and widths relevant to each other. Questions to ask include:

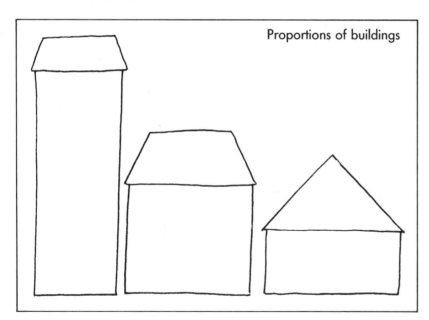

Proportions of buildings

- Is it a tall building?
- Is it single storey or multi-storey?
- Is it wide compared with its height?
- Does the roof slope steeply, or is it shallow pitched?
- What is the height of the roof compared with the height of the rest of the building?

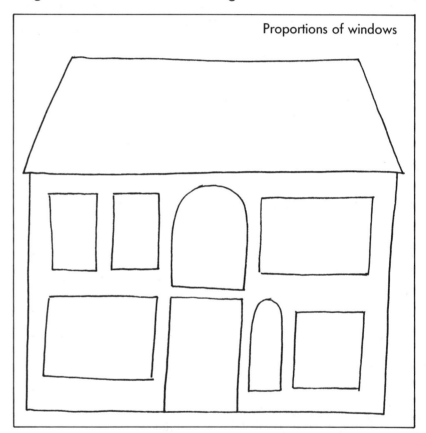

Proportions of windows

Once they have determined the proportions of the shell, encourage the children to go on to think about details, the most important being windows and doors. First, they should look at their size compared with the shell of the building, and at how they are positioned.

When these proportions have been determined, other details such as chimneys, window styles (for example sash or dormer), tiles and bricks can be considered. When all the above points have been discussed, encourage the children to draw, keeping the drawing process along the same lines as the discussion.

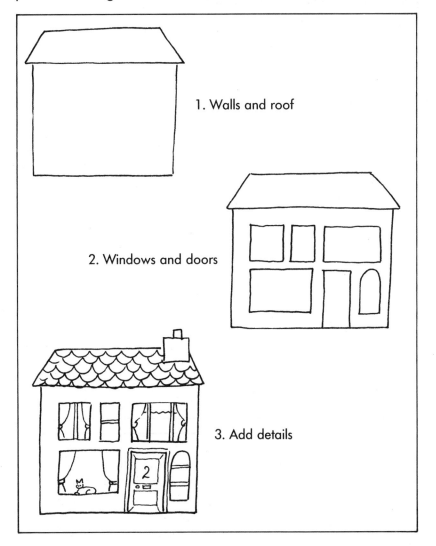

1. Walls and roof

2. Windows and doors

3. Add details

Self-portraits

Age range
Nine upwards.

Group size
Individuals.

What you need
Paper, soft pencils, crayons or pastels, hand-mirrors.

What to do
With the class, consider the basic shapes of faces (Figure 1). Ask the children to look at their own reflections and decide which basic shape is nearest to their own. They can then draw that shape using a light

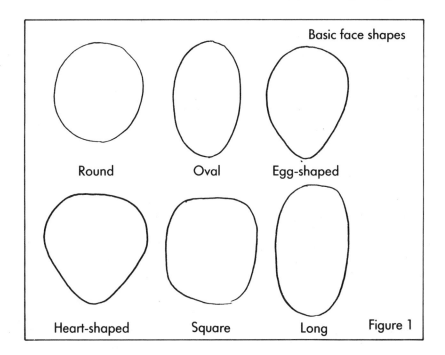

Basic face shapes

Round   Oval   Egg-shaped

Heart-shaped   Square   Long   Figure 1

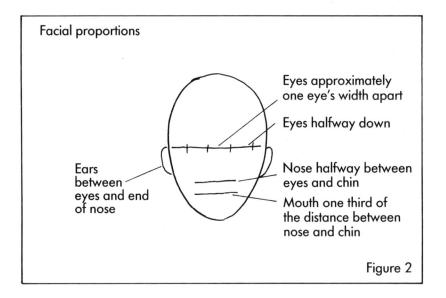

Facial proportions

Eyes approximately one eye's width apart

Eyes halfway down

Nose halfway between eyes and chin

Mouth one third of the distance between nose and chin

Ears between eyes and end of nose

Figure 2

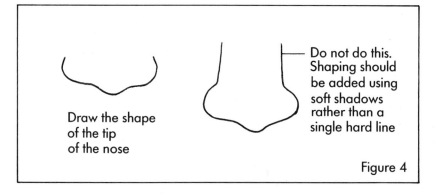

Draw the shape of the tip of the nose

Do not do this. Shaping should be added using soft shadows rather than a single hard line

Figure 4

pencil line.

Figure 2 shows the positioning of features in the average nine- to twelve-year-old. Ask the class to mark these positions faintly in pencil on their drawing. They should then check in the mirror to see whether these positions should be altered to suit their own faces; if so,

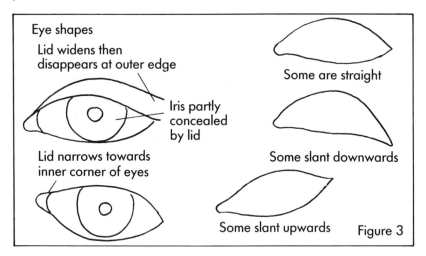

Eye shapes

Lid widens then disappears at outer edge

Iris partly concealed by lid

Lid narrows towards inner corner of eyes

Some are straight

Some slant downwards

Some slant upwards

Figure 3

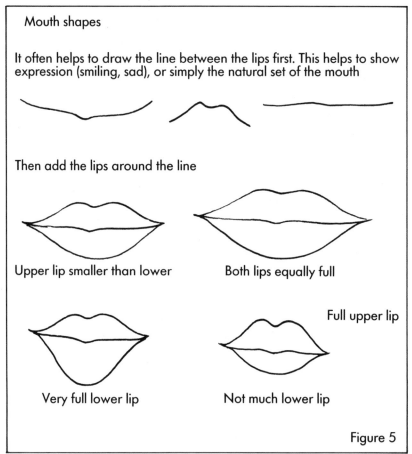

Mouth shapes

It often helps to draw the line between the lips first. This helps to show expression (smiling, sad), or simply the natural set of the mouth

Then add the lips around the line

Upper lip smaller than lower

Both lips equally full

Full upper lip

Very full lower lip

Not much lower lip

Figure 5

they should alter them at this stage.

Once the main construction lines are in place, let the children draw in the features in greater detail. Figures 3,

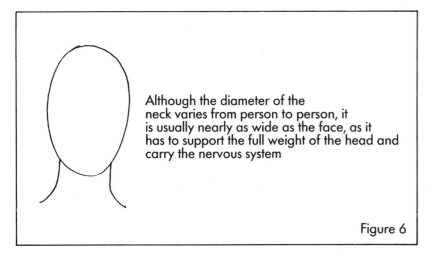

Although the diameter of the neck varies from person to person, it is usually nearly as wide as the face, as it has to support the full weight of the head and carry the nervous system

Figure 6

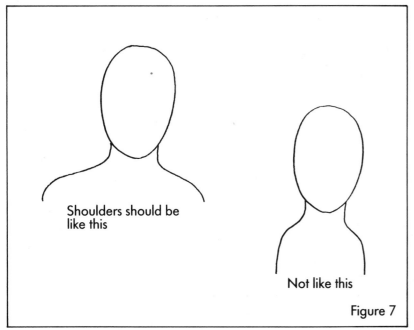

Shoulders should be like this

Not like this

Figure 7

4 and 5 show different facial features. Hair, neck and shoulders can then be added as in Figures 6, 7 and 8.

When all the features have been 'mapped' in with faint pencil lines, the portrait can be completed using colour. Skin tones can be achieved by mixing colours and using light, slanting strokes with pastel or crayon. Encourage the children to experiment on scrap paper to find the best combination of colours to represent their own skin tones.

Form can be suggested by adding shadows using darker tones, still employing slanting strokes of pastel

Draw in the shape of the mass of hair, then add details of direction, curls and so on

Figure 8

or crayon.

To suggest hair, apply crayon or pastel in lines which follow the direction of the hair style, again using a blend of colours as this gives a much more natural effect. NB: The proportions of the average nine- to twelve-year-old's face are as shown in Figure 2. However, there are very few children who fit that pattern exactly, and it is the ways in which individuals differ from the average which distinguish them from each other. It is useful to know what the mythical 'average' is, because it can be used as a frame of reference against which to measure the real proportions.

Drawing still life

Age range
Nine upwards.

Group size
Individuals.

What you need
Vase(s) of flowers (jam jars will do), paper, soft pencils, pastels, crayons or paint.

What to do
Ask the children to look carefully at the subject, and then make a 'plan' of it to show the relative positions and sizes of the individual components (Figure 1). Each

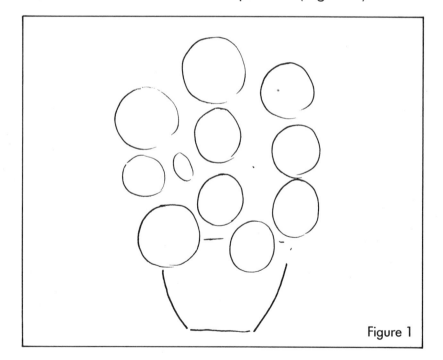

Figure 1

child's plan will, of course, be slightly different, as each will have a different view.

When the plans are complete, let the children add details of shape and colour (Figure 2) using their chosen

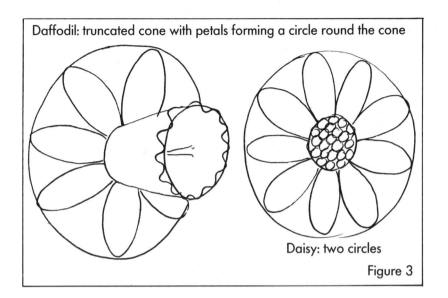

Daffodil: truncated cone with petals forming a circle round the cone

Daisy: two circles

Figure 3

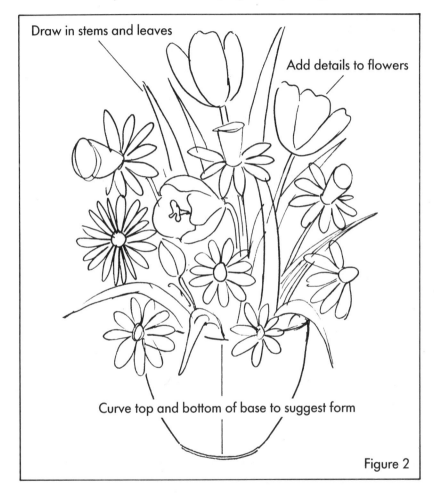

Draw in stems and leaves

Add details to flowers

Curve top and bottom of base to suggest form

Figure 2

medium. Older children should be encouraged to construct the flowers as in Figure 3, as this is an exercise in representational drawing. Any construction lines should be drawn very faintly, so that they can be

adjusted without spoiling the finished picture and will not show through the colour. Colour should be applied following the directions of the forms, as in Figure 4.

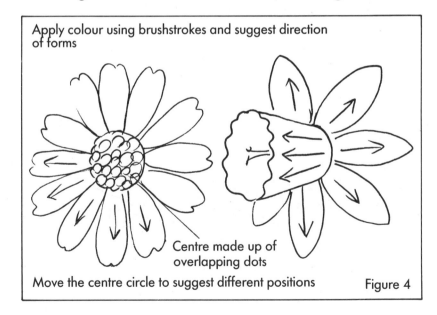

Apply colour using brushstrokes and suggest direction of forms

Centre made up of overlapping dots

Move the centre circle to suggest different positions

Figure 4

Giant food models

Age range
Eleven to twelve.

Group size
Pairs, threes or fours.

What you need
Scrap materials (such as newspaper, cardboard boxes, egg cartons and fabric), paint, paste, paper, drawing materials, copies of photocopiable page 113.

What to do
The aim of this activity is to introduce modelling from junk materials and to help the children to understand the importance of following instructions and planning.

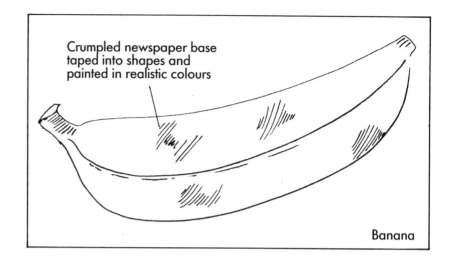

Crumpled newspaper base taped into shapes and painted in realistic colours

Banana

Introduce the theme of food and explain that the children are going to make giant models of food, like those used in promotion, or in a theatre or television production. If possible, show the class pictures of food sculptures by Claus Oldenburg and other artists, and discuss any giant models which the class may have seen.

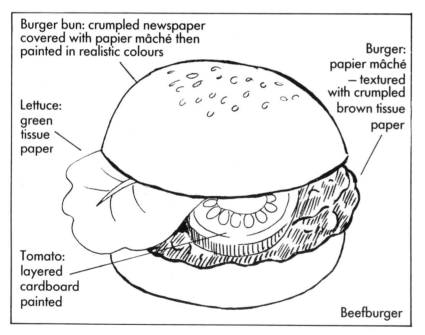

Burger bun: crumpled newspaper covered with papier mâché then painted in realistic colours

Burger: papier mâché — textured with crumpled brown tissue paper

Lettuce: green tissue paper

Tomato: layered cardboard painted

Beefburger

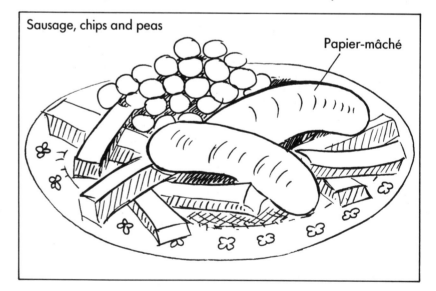

Sausage, chips and peas

Papier-mâché

String pattern

Custard cream

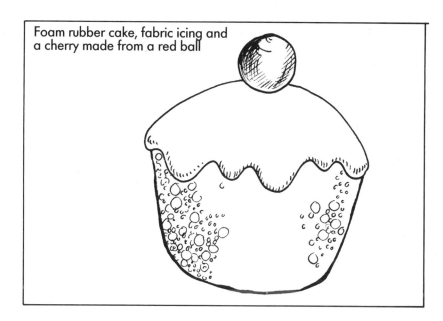

Foam rubber cake, fabric icing and a cherry made from a red ball

Discuss the materials the children have available, and the techniques with which they are already familiar and which might be useful in this project. Divide the class into groups of not more than four, then ask them to decide what food items to make, and how to make them.

Each child should then make out a worksheet, either using photocopiable page 113 or devising their own, detailing what is to be made, with step-by-step

instructions on how to make it. These should be checked to ensure that every child knows what he has to do, making comments and adjustments if necessary. A list of required materials should be made, to help with organisation. This will also help to encourage the children to take responsibility for their work, rather than leaving everything to you. When all the preparations have been completed, let the children make their models.

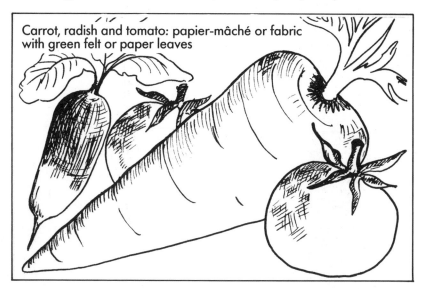

Carrot, radish and tomato: papier-mâché or fabric with green felt or paper leaves

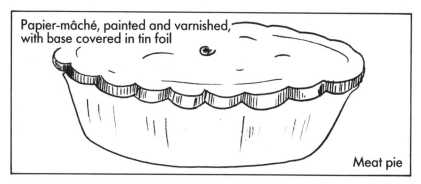

Papier-mâché, painted and varnished, with base covered in tin foil

Meat pie

Basic techniques

The wide range of activities in this chapter introduces children to a variety of materials, tools and techniques, such as marbling, tie-dyeing, stencilling and printing. Most of them are used elsewhere in the book, and where relevant, are cross-referenced back to this chapter.

Where a design is needed to decorate an item such as a piece of pottery or felt, observational drawings can be used. Alternatively, a geometric pattern could be used, such as patterns made with crayon resist (see Patterns-Crayon resist pattern, page 77).

Some of the activities in this chapter require the use of a template and there is a selection at the back of the book which can be photocopied.

Resist painting

Age range
Five upwards.

Group size
Individuals.

What you need
Wax crayons, paper, paint, pencils.

What to do
Ask the children to make several drawings of a specific subject. This could be linked with a current project, or chosen specifically for this activity. With young children, choose something very simple such as a daisy-type flower or a box-type building. Ask the children to choose one of their drawings and go over the lines in wax crayon. They should then paint over this with water-based paint using a contrasting colour. The wax will resist the paint and produce an interesting grainy effect.

This is the basic principle behind other resist techniques such as batik and lithography.

Marbled beads

Age range
Five upwards.

Group size
Individuals.

What you need
Self-hardening clay in two contrasting colours, knitting needle, varnish, thin wire.

What to do
Ask each child to roll together small amounts of self-hardening clay in two contrasting colours until a marbled pattern begins to appear. Ask them to roll the clay into bead shapes.

Let the children carefully pierce each bead with a knitting needle, then leave them to dry.

When the beads are dry, thread them on to thin wire then cover them in varnish to seal the surface.

Follow-up
Encourage the children to make a simple abacus with their beads.

Plaster casts

Age range
Five upwards (with adult help).

Group size
Individuals.

What you need
Small items such as sea shells, walnut shells or anything with a compact shape and some sort of detailing, plaster of Paris, clay, paints, brushes.

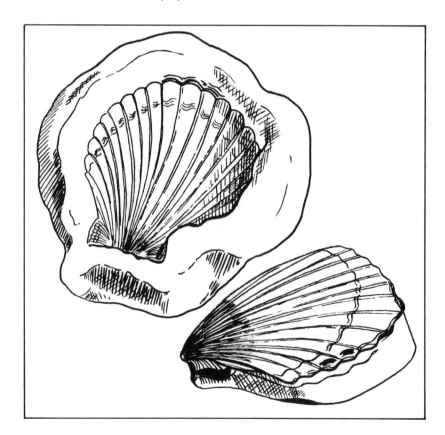

What to do

This activity demonstrates the basic process of making a mould.

Encourage the children to press the items into a lump of clay to make a clear impression.

Mix the plaster according to the manufacturer's instructions. It should then be poured into the simple moulds.

Allow the plaster to dry completely (preferably overnight) before removing the models from the mould, and giving them to the children to paint. These could then be used in collage work or as Christmas tree decorations.

Cut paper patterns

Age range
Six upwards.

Group size
Individuals.

What you need
A variety of coloured paper, scissors, pencils, paper for the background in a contrasting colour (or black or white), adhesive.

What to do
Ask the children to draw one or more shapes in pencil and cut round them to make templates. Let them draw round them several times on different coloured sheets of paper. Cut out the coloured shapes and let the children arrange them on the backing paper to make a repeat pattern, then stick them in place.

Different arrangements using the same shapes can be created and different colour combinations can be tried out.

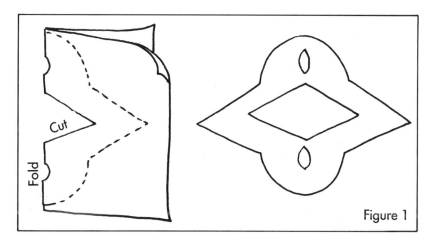

Figure 1

Older children can make more sophisticated patterns by folding a piece of paper in half and cutting out a shape with holes as in Figure 1. This can then be used as a template, with perhaps another shape being used as an infill as in Figure 2.

Figure 2

Monoprint greetings cards

Age range
Six upwards.

Group size
Individuals.

What you need
Folded cartridge paper for cards, paint in squeezy bottles, pencils, newspaper.

What to do
Invite the children to draw a design in pencil on a sheet of folded cartridge paper. Make sure that there is plenty of space between the pencil marks, because if they are too close together, when a print is taken, the paint will splurge uncontrollably. (It is a good idea to let the children practise on newspaper if they have not used this technique before.)

Figure 2

Ask the children to go over the pencil marks with paint as in Figure 1, then carefully place a sheet of newspaper over the design, smoothing it over to ensure contact with the paint (Figure 2). The newspaper should then be peeled off.

Ask each child to look at the original and decide either to leave it as it is, or to add to it. If they want to add to it, let them apply further paint to the original, and use a fresh sheet of newspaper to 'blot' it. They can add more paint as many times as they like, but fresh paper must be used every time they 'blot' it, to avoid smudging.

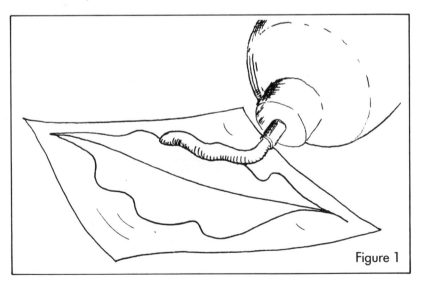

Figure 1

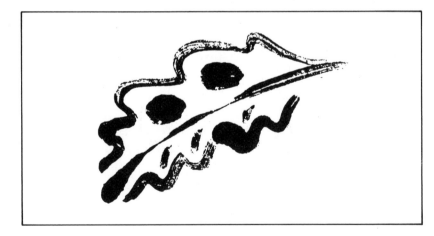

Thumb pot

Age range
Six upwards.

Group size
Individuals.

What you need
Clay, improvised tools (such as an old table fork or comb), paints.

What to do
Wedge the clay and let the children form it into balls small enough to fit comfortably in their hands (orange size for older children, clementine size for younger ones). They shouldn't handle the clay unnecessarily, as heat from their hands will dry it out and make it crack.

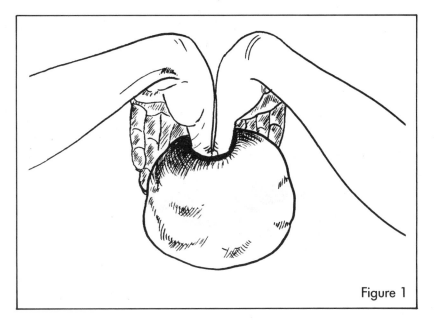

Figure 1

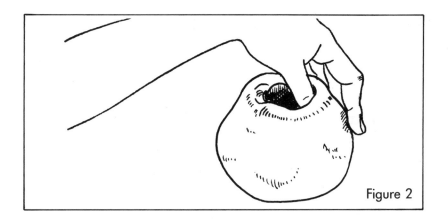

Figure 2

To start the pot, encourage the children to press their thumbs into each ball of clay to make a deep hole (Figure 1). Then they should carefully pinch the walls of the pot to make them thinner (Figure 2). Ensure that they keep turning the pot as they do this. They should try to keep the hole at the top of the pot as small as possible, because if it widens too soon, the walls will flop, and they will be left with a saucer instead of a hollow pot!

Older children will be able to make a fairly thin-walled pot, but younger ones will probably only manage a thick-sided one.

Let the children decorate their pots with a scratched (sgraffito) pattern, using the improvised tools, and allow them to paint them if they wish.

Stick pot

Age range
Six upwards.

Group size
Individuals.

What you need
Clay, pieces of dowel, clay modelling tools.

What to do
Ask the children to prepare the clay by wedging it and roughly shaping it into cubes. Let each child make a hole by pressing into the cube with a piece of dowel (Figure 1). They should not press too far, or the pot will be bottomless!

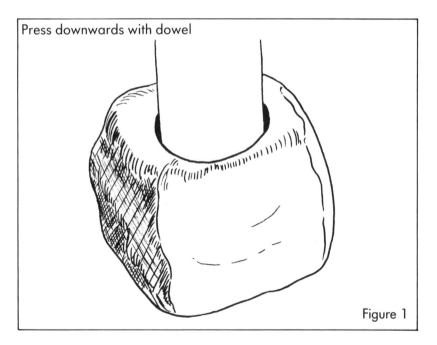

Press downwards with dowel

Figure 1

Visual interest can be added to the pot by carving patterns into the sides using modelling tools. Objects such as coins or buttons can also make an impressed pattern. These pots are meant to look chunky and robust, so don't worry too much about perfect shapes.

Painted beads

Age range
Seven upwards.

Group size
Individuals.

What you need
Self-hardening clay, knitting needles, paint, brushes, varnish, thin wire, Plasticine.

What to do
Let the children roll the clay into balls in the palms of their hands. Ask them to make a hole through each one using a knitting needle.

Allow the beads to dry thoroughly, then let the children paint them in plain colours, resting the knitting needle on lumps of Plasticine so that the beads can turn freely, as in Figure 1. Once the first layer of paint has

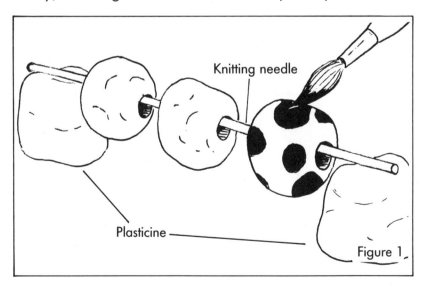

Figure 1

dried, the children can go on to paint on patterns in contrasting colours. When dry, the beads can be varnished to seal the surface and give the beads a shine.

Once the varnish has dried, let the children thread the beads on to thin wire.

Follow-up
Let the children use their beads to decorate pieces of embroidery. Remind them that the beads must be removed if the item is to be washed.

Printing shapes

Age range
Seven upwards (or five if pre-cut shapes are available).

Group size
Individuals or pairs.

What you need
Copies of photocopiable page 114 (optional), corrugated card, pencils, paper, scissors, sugar paper, paint, paint brushes, foam rubber or sponge (optional).

What to do
Ask the children to practise drawing Paisley shapes on paper first, and then to draw one on corrugated card. (Young children can use copies of photocopiable page 114 as a template.) Cut it out, and apply paint to one side using a brush. More than one colour can be applied at once provided that a gap is left between colours to prevent runs (Figure 1). Let the children turn the card shape, painted face down, to the sugar paper,

and press gently but firmly. They can then re-apply paint, and repeat to make a pattern (Figure 2). This can also be done with more than one card shape. The

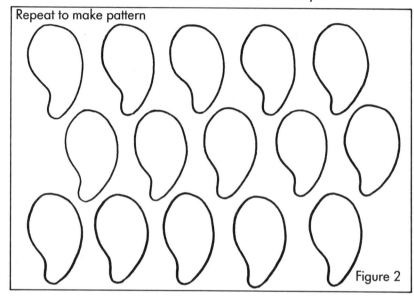

Repeat to make pattern

Figure 2

shapes can be alternated to make a more complicated pattern (Figure 3).

Foam rubber or sponge can be used instead of cardboard to make the printing shapes; they will give a different texture, but the principle is the same.

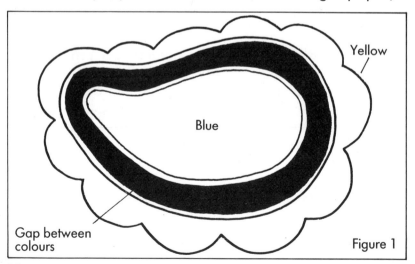

Yellow

Blue

Gap between colours

Figure 1

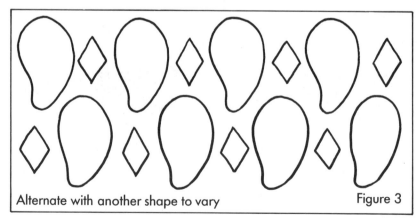

Alternate with another shape to vary

Figure 3

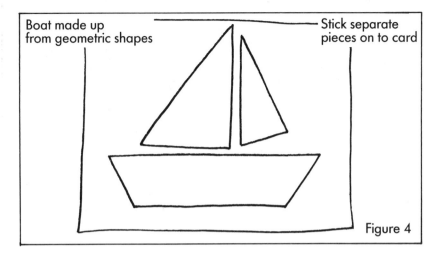

Boat made up from geometric shapes

Stick separate pieces on to card

Figure 4

Follow-up

Let the children develop this basic technique by building up pictures to print. For example, a boat image could be built up by sticking geometric shapes on to a piece of card, as in Figure 4. Alternatively, the basic shape could be developed once the print has been made, as in Figure 5.

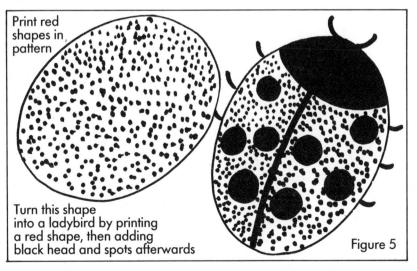

Print red shapes in pattern

Turn this shape into a ladybird by printing a red shape, then adding black head and spots afterwards

Figure 5

Butterflying

Age range
Seven upwards.

Group size
Individuals.

What you need
Symmetrical objects (such as apples, leaves, cockle shells, or man-made items), drawing paper, sugar paper, paint, brushes.

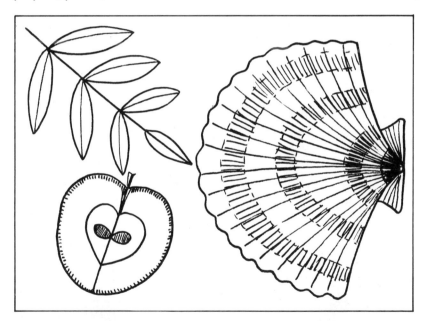

What to do
Working as a whole class, choose an object and study it, making sketches to show its shape, distinctive markings and other characteristics. Ask the children to mark the centre of their drawings with a line.

Let each child fold a piece of sugar paper in half and, using paint, begin to copy half of one of their sketches (Figure 1). This should be done a little at a time, re-folding the sugar paper along the centre line and blotting each application of paint, thus building up a

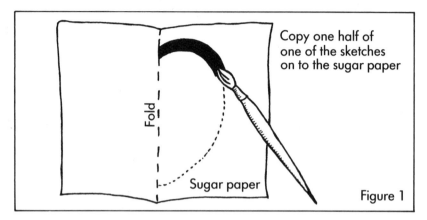

Copy one half of one of the sketches on to the sugar paper

Fold

Sugar paper

Figure 1

symmetrical design. The children shouldn't let the paint dry too much, as it will make a poor impression when blotted. If they use paint from a squeezy bottle instead of using a brush, the results will be more difficult to control, but let them try each method separately or use a combination of the two in the same painting.

Stencilled cards

Age range
Seven upwards.

Group size
Pairs.

What you need
Simple objects to work from (leaves, flowers, cockle shells), drawing paper, pencils, paper for stencils, scissors, cartridge or sugar paper for cards, paint, stencil brushes or stiff hogshair brushes.

What to do
Ask the children to make simple drawings of the subject, as in Figure 1.

Figure 1

The drawings should then be adapted for use as stencil designs by folding the stencil paper and drawing on half of the design in pencil around the fold line, as in

Figure 2. Ask the children to cut carefully along the line and unfold the paper.

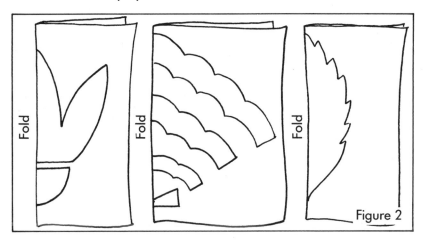

Figure 2

Ask the children to work in pairs, one holding the stencil steady while the other uses the stiff brush to apply paint over the stencil and on to the card. Encourage them to take turns in holding the stencil. Show the children how to apply the paint using a stippling or dabbing technique, preferably working from the outside edges of the stencil towards the centre.

Encourage the children to use more than one colour to fill in each stencil shape as this will give a more subtle textured effect.

Positive/negative images

Age range
Seven upwards.

Group size
Individuals.

What you need
Sugar paper in two contrasting colours, scissors, adhesive, spreaders, pencils.

What to do
Allow each child to choose one of the classic motifs shown here or to design one of her own.

Give each child four pieces of paper, two of each colour, for example, black and white. Ask the children to take one piece of each colour, place them together,

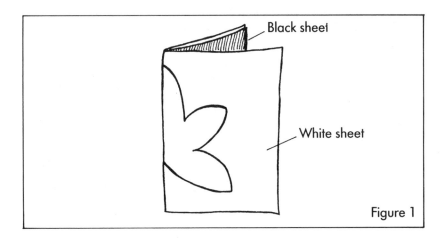

Black sheet

White sheet

Figure 1

and fold them together down the centre. Half of the design should be drawn on one side of the fold as in Figure 1. The shape can then be cut out from both pieces

Figure 2

of paper simultaneously. Discard the edges of the paper and stick the white shape(s) to the second black piece of paper and vice versa, as in Figure 2.

30

String-printed art folder

Age range
Seven upwards.

Group size
Individuals.

What you need
Large sheets of sugar paper, corrugated card, scissors, string of various types, PVA adhesive, spreaders, paint, brushes, a stapler, scrap paper.

What to do
Make up the printing 'blocks' at least a day before they are needed, so that the adhesive has ample time to dry. To make the blocks, ask the children to cut pieces of corrugated card approximately 10cm square, cover one side with PVA adhesive and arrange string on it,

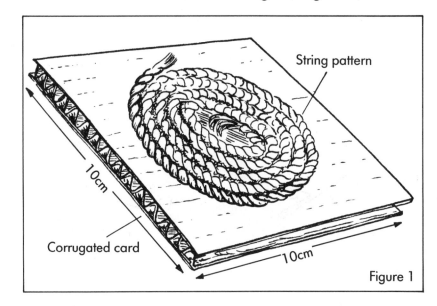

String pattern

10cm

Corrugated card

10cm

Figure 1

bending and shaping it to make different patterns (Figure 1). Ensure that they hold it in place for a few minutes until the adhesive begins to dry. Make sure that the children realise that strings of different thicknesses should not be mixed on one block, because only the thickest string will produce an impression.

When the children are ready to print, let them apply paint to the string using a brush, and take some test prints on scrap paper. Make sure they know that moving the block will distort the image, so they must hold it lightly, but firmly, in place, and carefully apply pressure to achieve a bold impression.

Let them experiment on scrap paper to work out a repeat pattern, then print on to the sugar paper.

When the printing is thoroughly dry, help the children to make up the folder as shown in Figure 2.

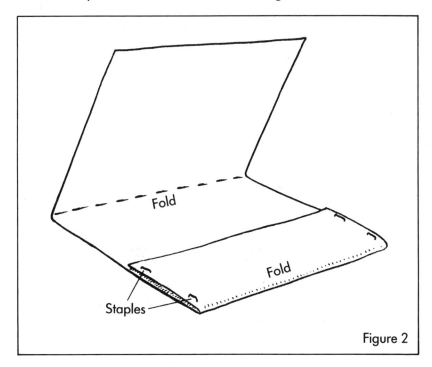

Fold

Fold

Staples

Figure 2

Tie-dyed fabric

Age range
Eight upwards (with adult help).

Group size
Individuals or pairs.

What you need
Cotton fabric (not polycotton or mercerised), cold water, fibre-reactive dyes (such as Dylon), string, washing soda, salt.

What to do
New fabric may contain dressing, and this needs to be removed by washing as it may inhibit the uptake of dye. If the fabric is washed, make sure that it is completely dry before beginning work.

Explain to the children how tie-dye is a 'resist' technique in which the fabric is tightly bound to control the uptake of dye. A variety of patterns can be made by folding or scrunching the fabric in different ways before it is tied with string. Different patterns can be combined in the same piece of work, but it is a good idea to

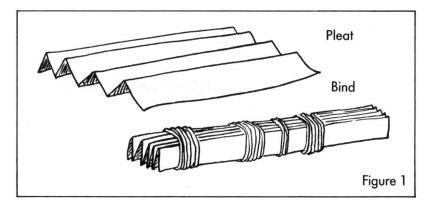

Pleat

Bind

Figure 1

experiment first by making up a set of samples; it is much easier to plan a pattern if you know what results are possible, and how to achieve them. Here are some suggestions for binding which the children can try out:

● Fold the fabric to make pleats, and tie it at intervals (Figure 1).

● Gather the fabric together into a long sausage shape, and bind it at intervals (Figure 2).

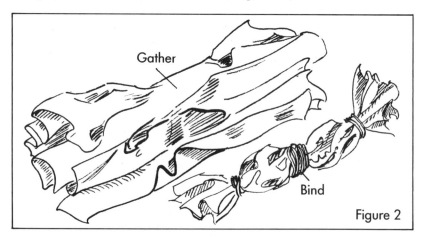

Figure 2

● Scrunch the fabric into a ball, and bind it so that it stays in a tight ball, while gaps remain between the string (Figure 3).

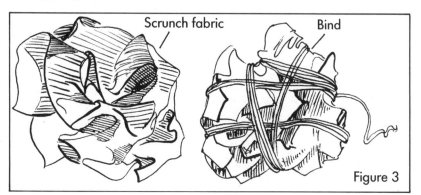

Figure 3

● Place pebbles on the fabric at intervals and tie them into the fabric (Figure 4). This will give a circular pattern.

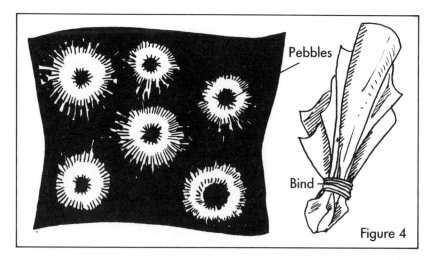

Figure 4

● Tie knots in the fabric (Figure 5) (but don't pull them so tight that they can't be undone!).

Tie-dyed fabric can be used to make tote-bags and bean-bags. In addition, it can be used in collage work or appliqué, or pinned to notice boards to make an attractive background for a display.

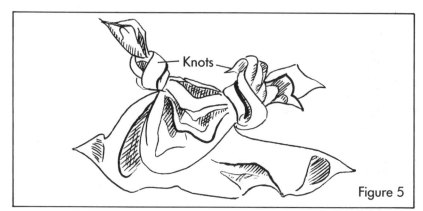

Figure 5

Moulded clay dish

Age range
Eight upwards.

Group size
Individuals.

What you need
Plaster dish moulds, clay, rolling pins, batons or dowels, cutting and trimming tools, damp sponge, kiln (optional), paint, brushes.

What to do
Help the children to prepare the clay and roll it out, placing it between two batons or dowels to ensure that it is a uniform width. The thickness required will depend on the size of the mould; the larger the mould, the thicker the clay – up to 1cm thick for a 30cm dish. Carefully transfer the clay from the work surface to the mould, as if making a pastry case. Let the children smooth it gently into place so that it fits right into the mould and then trim the edges. The plaster will absorb water from the clay, and the dish will dry quite quickly at room temperature. It can be removed from the mould when leather-hard, allowing someone else a turn!

Use a damp sponge to smooth any rough edges, and then, if necessary, fire the dish.

Let the children paint it with a geometric design or use a design developed from observational drawings of natural objects.

Paper folding

Age range
Eight upwards.

Group size
Individuals.

What you need
Squares of tissue paper, scissors, large sheets of paper in contrasting colours.

What to do
Show the children various ways of folding a square of paper, as in Figure 1, and how to make cuts in the

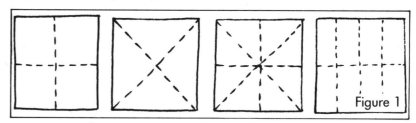

Figure 1

folded square. Show them what happens when the square is unfolded (Figure 2). Encourage the children to experiment with folding and cutting the paper in different ways.

Display the results on large sheets of paper of a contrasting colour.

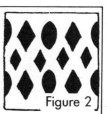

Figure 2

Paper weaving

Age range
Eight upwards.

Group size
Individuals.

What you need
Sheets of plain paper in a variety of contrasting colours, rulers, pencils, scissors.

What to do
Ask the children to fold a sheet of paper in half and use a ruler and pencil to mark on a series of parallel lines as shown in Figure 1. Let them cut along the lines as shown, and explain that these will form the warp of their weaving.

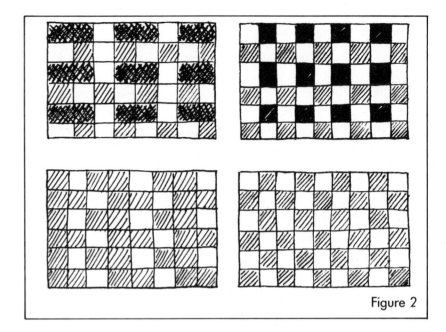

Figure 2

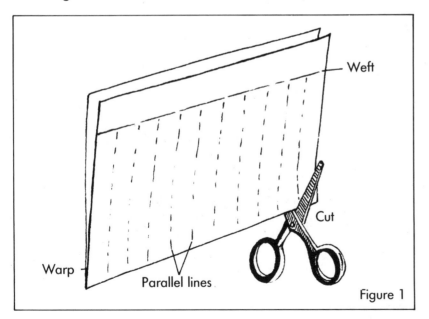

Figure 1

Allow the children to select pieces of paper in contrasting colours and cut them into strips. Explain that these will form the weft and show them different ways of weaving as in Figure 2. Encourage them to experiment using different weaves and different colours.

Design a tile

Age range
Nine upwards.

Group size
Individuals.

What you need
Clay, batons, rolling pins, tile cutter, clay modelling tools, overalls, paint, brushes.

What to do

Before the activity, ask the children to make a design on paper for a tile. When the designs are finished ask the children to prepare the clay and roll it out to a thickness of approximately 2cm. They can then cut out a tile using a template or tile cutter.

Let the children make some thin coils of clay by rolling them between the palms of their hands. Ask them to cut out flat shapes from thinner pieces of clay to make a visual contrast.

Let them lay the shapes in place on top of the tile, piece by piece, fixing them in place by using a round-ended tool and carefully scraping a small amount of clay off the side of the shape and down on to the tile as in Figure 1.

When the decorated tile is dry, the children can smooth away any roughness using a damp sponge. Tiles like this can also be made using dough.

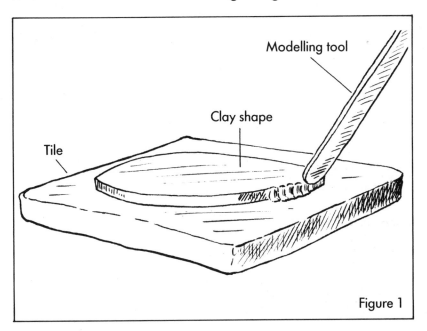

Modelling tool

Clay shape

Tile

Figure 1

Felt picture

Age range
Nine upwards.

Group size
Individuals.

What you need
Felting noils, coloured wool tops, scraps of knitting yarn, net curtaining, rolling pins or wooden dowels, string, diluted washing-up liquid in a squeezy bottle.

What to do
Show the children how to lay pieces of net flat on the work surface. The net should be large enough to wrap around the picture they are about to make. Let the children arrange the coloured wool tops and yarn in a pattern or motif on the net (Figure 1). Encourage them to

Net

Pattern or picture
Leave sufficient net to wrap around picture

Figure 1

use the yarn for making outlines, and pull the wool tops into thin tufts, so that they can be used to make solid areas of colour, or can be manipulated to make thick outlines.

Next, give the children felting noils and show them how to pull them into thin tufts and make a layer covering the coloured pattern, as in Figure 2. Ask them

Figure 2

Cover the first layer with a second layer of fibres. These should lie in the opposite direction

Figure 3

to put another layer of noils over the first, but this time the tufts must lie in the opposite direction to those in the first layer (Figure 3). Add up to three more layers, in alternate directions.

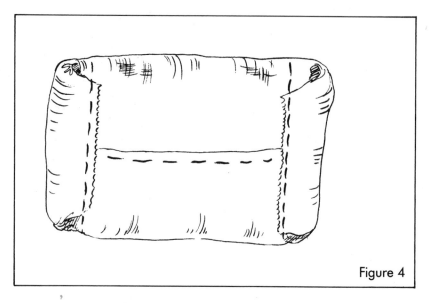

Figure 4

Ask the children to check that there is no light showing through the noils, then fold the edges of the net over them to make a parcel (Figure 4). If necessary, this can be secured with a few stitches.

Show the children how to wrap the parcel around a rolling pin, making sure that it is not loose, then bind it with string to secure everything in position (Figure 5).

Let the children squirt washing-up liquid over the bundle so that it is wet, but not dripping. Then get them to roll it backwards and forwards across a hard surface, as though rolling out pastry, but using more pressure. Continue this rolling for at least 20 minutes. It is easy to tell when the fleece is beginning to felt, because it feels firmer, and fibres begin to penetrate the net. At this point, let the children open out the parcel to check

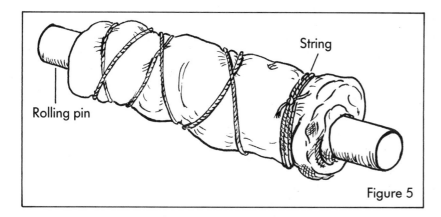

Rolling pin

String

Figure 5

progress. If the fleece is not felted, continue the process. Felt can be left on the rolling pin overnight, and given a further rolling the next day. This does, in fact, help the felting process.

When the felt is ready, ask the children to rinse it carefully in warm water to remove the washing-up liquid, then dry it flat, or on a radiator.

Marbled paper

Age range
Nine upwards (with adult help).

Group size
Individuals.

What you need
Oil paint, white spirit or turpentine substitute, rubber gloves, overalls, strong paper such as cartridge paper, a water bath (a sink or large, but shallow, plastic container).

What to do
Mix the oil paint with white spirit to the consistency of milk. Pour a little of the mixture into a shallow bath of water and allow it to swirl around and form patterns. Add drops of another colour in selected places and allow them to mingle with the first. More colours may be added if required, but preferably not more than four in total.

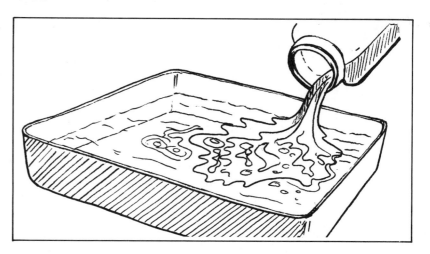

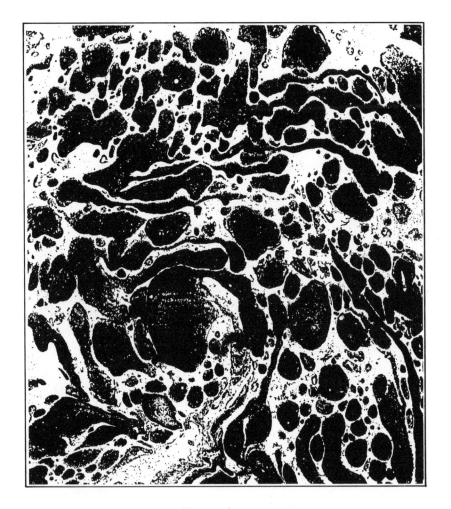

When the paint has formed an attractive pattern on the surface of the water, allow the children to place sheets of paper face down on it. The paper should then be lifted out carefully, and laid flat on newspaper to dry. Add more spots of colour to the water as necessary.

When dry, the paper can be used for covering books and pencil pot holders, making paper fans and mobiles. NB: Oil paint can be extremely messy if not used carefully and is difficult to remove from clothing.

Tessellations 1

Age range
Nine upwards.

Group size
Individuals.

What you need
Copies of photocopiable pages 115 and 116, paper, scissors, pencils, felt-tipped pens.

What to do
Ask the children to draw round the templates on photocopiable pages 115 and 116 to make a tessellated grid pattern. Older or more able children could make their own templates from thin card.

When the grid is complete, let the children design a motif to fit into a single shape and which can be repeated in the grid to make a complex shape. Examples are given in the illustration below.

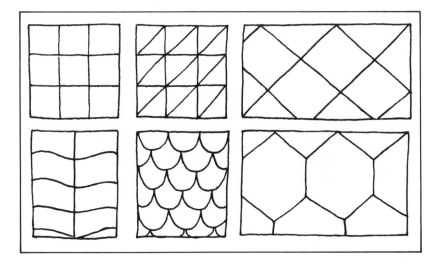

Tessellations 2

Age range
Nine upwards.

Group size
Individuals.

What you need
Copies of photocopiable pages 115 and 116, paper, pencils, felt-tipped pen, scissors, sponge wipes, small blocks of wood, adhesive, paint, margarine tubs.

What to do
Let the children experiment with tessellating shapes using copies of photocopiable pages 115 and 116. If they wish, let them cut into the edges of their shapes, as in Figure 1, but explain that the shapes must be able to tessellate. Encourage them to make designs that are striking, but fairly simple, and to make a rough sketch on paper.

When they have achieved suitable designs, ask them to place their chosen template on to a sponge wipe and to draw round it in felt-tipped pen. Let them cut out the sponge shapes and ask them to stick on a block of wood to act as a handle (Figure 2).

Figure 2

Give the children margarine tubs of paint and show them how to use their printers to make a tessellated pattern, following their original designs (Figure 3). Remind them to blot their printers carefully if they wish to use more than one colour.

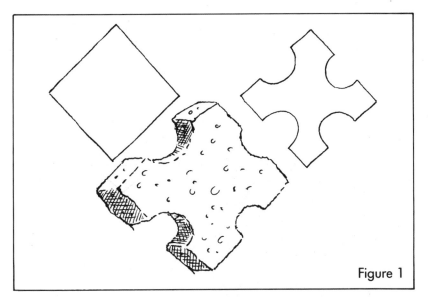

Figure 1

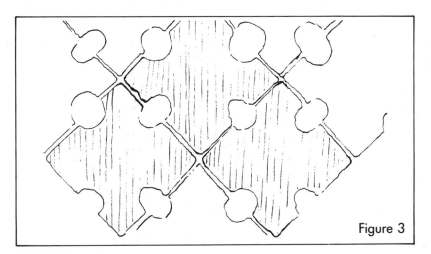

Figure 3

Freestanding plaster form

Age range
Ten upwards (with adult help).

Group size
Pairs.

What you need
An assortment of small cardboard boxes such as Toblerone or toothpaste boxes, tubes such as the barrels of old ballpoint pens and other scrap items, plaster of Paris, mixing bowls, clay or Plasticine to form base, paint (metallic is very effective, but be sure to use a non-toxic brand).

What to do
Encourage the children to form the clay or Plasticine into a domed lump and poke the tubes, boxes and other scrap items into it to make a dramatic arrangement (Figure 1). As a general rule, this can be achieved by

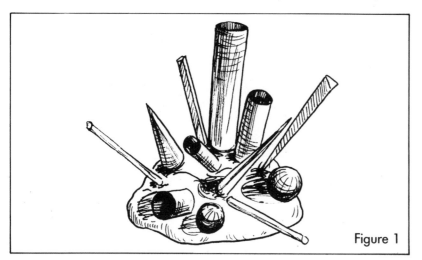

Figure 1

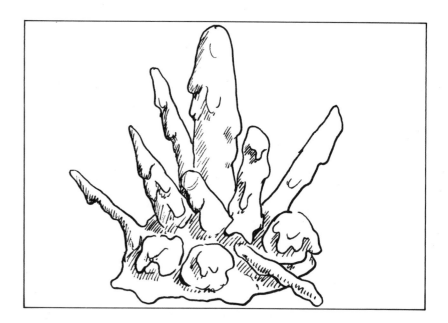

choosing a tall item for the focal point, placing it either in the centre of the base or at the back, then working round it or in front of it, whichever is applicable, using shorter items.

When the children are satisfied with their arrangements, they should cover them with a layer of plaster.

The plaster should be mixed by an adult, to the consistency of thick cream or custard. Make sure that all work surfaces where the plaster is to be used are well covered with newspaper. Do not mix the plaster until all the children are ready to use it, as it hardens very quickly. For this reason, do not wash out the bowls in the sink, or it may become blocked; instead, allow any residue to dry in the bowl, then knock it out on to newspaper, wrap it and throw it away.

Although plaster dries very quickly, it is better to allow at least a day for it to become completely dry, when it can be painted.

Plastering scrap

Age range
Ten upwards (with adult help).

Group size
Individuals, pairs or fours.

What you need
Clay, plaster of Paris, mixing bowls for the plaster, scrap items such as large nuts and bolts, cog wheels, cotton reels, ping-pong balls, paint or shoe polish.

What to do
Let the children roll out a piece of clay to a depth of about 3cm and then another piece 1cm deep. This second piece should then be cut into 6cm wide strips. Ask the children to use this to build a wall around the first piece of clay, sealing the joint with thin coils of clay as in Figure 1.

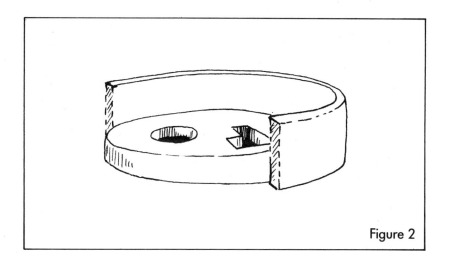

Figure 2

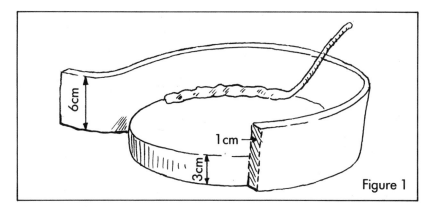

Figure 1

Let the children use the scrap items to make impressions of varying depths in the base of the clay mould; they should be careful not to go right through the clay (Figure 2). Check the moulds to ensure that all the joints are plaster-proof.

The plaster should then be mixed by an adult, according to the manufacturer's instructions, and poured slowly into the moulds, almost to the top of the clay walls.

Allow at least 24 hours for the plaster to dry out, then remove the clay (this can be re-used for mould-making, but not for pottery). Make sure that all traces of clay are removed from the reliefs, then let the children paint them or treat them with shoe polish.

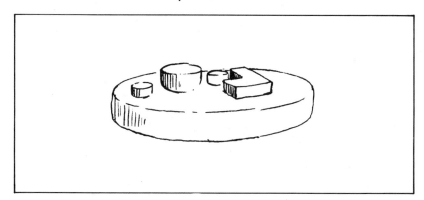

Making pictures

Creating a picture is not always a matter of just using pencils and paints. The activities suggested in this chapter will help children to create pictures using a variety of materials and techniques, such as collage and printing. The suggestions given allow ample room for the children to use their imagination and to express themselves individually.

When making pictures, sketchpads are useful for initial rough sketches, while scrapbooks containing a variety of pictures and photographs are useful reference sources, whether the subject is real or imaginary. Careful use of colours should always be encouraged.

Fish tank

Age range
Five upwards.

Group size
Individuals.

What you need
Sugar paper or kitchen paper, paints, brushes.

What to do
Many schools have a tank of fish, and they make an ideal subject for a painting. Begin by looking carefully with the children at the tank and its contents. Ask the children questions about the shapes and colours of the fish and draw some basic shapes on the chalkboard. Discuss the water plants too, and any rocks, stones or shells in the tank.

Ask the children to paint the basic shapes directly on to sugar paper using paint of a similar colour to that of the paper. They should draw the shape of the tank first, then add rocks, plants and fish, overlapping shapes just as they really appear to overlap. When the sketch is complete, let the children paint in details using colours mixed to match the real colours.

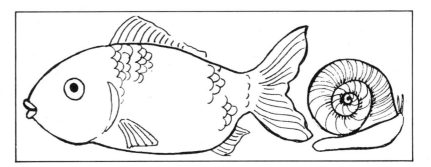

A dragon collage

Age range
Five upwards.

Group size
Individuals, pairs or fours (depending on the size of the picture).

What you need
Sugar paper, adhesive, spreaders, scissors, scrap materials (such as milk bottle tops, sweet wrappers, foil, egg trays or cartons, fruit nets), pictures of dragons and lizards.

What to do
With the class, read and discuss some stories about dragons and look at pictures of imaginary dragons and photographs of lizards. Compare the pictures and photographs for points of similarity, such as scales, horns, and writhing serpent-like bodies. Some lizards have crests or huge leathery 'collars' which look very dragon-like; others have long tongues. Many reptiles have exotic colouring and some are very brightly patterned.

Show the children the scrap materials available, and discuss how these could be used: for example, milk bottle tops in various colours could be used to suggest scales. Discarded sweet wrappers could be cut into scale shapes or stuck together to make a patchwork pattern. Egg cartons could be cut up and used to represent bumps.

After the discussion, ask the children to make their own pictures of dragons. Let them draw outlines in pencil if they wish, then encourage them to use the materials as discussed. Each dragon should almost fill the picture space.

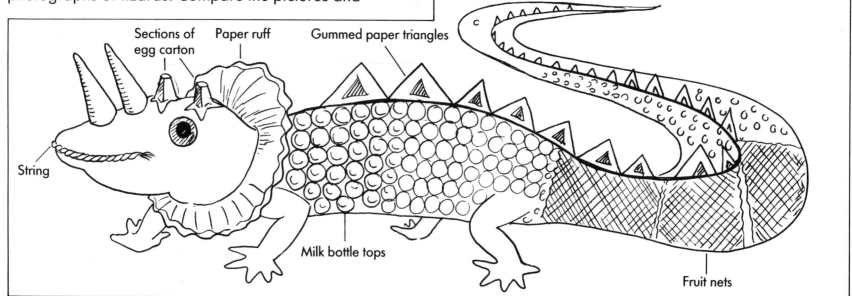

Sections of egg carton   Paper ruff   Gummed paper triangles

String

Milk bottle tops

Fruit nets

Circus frieze

Age range
Six upwards.

Group size
Whole class.

What you need
Frieze paper, pieces of paper, crayons or paint, reference material.

What to do
Although many children are not able to visit a real circus, many will have seen circuses on television. The best time to do this activity would be after Christmas when circus programmes are often screened. Showing the children a video recording of a circus would be very helpful. Photographs of circus acts are useful too.

As a class, discuss the people involved in the acts, what they looked like, what they wore and what they did.

Then ask each child to choose a subject, and to draw it in paint or crayon, preferably from memory. Ask the children to cut round their pictures when they are ready, and then to arrange them on the frieze paper, juggling the shapes round to find the most attractive arrangement. Shapes can be overlapped if required.

Rock pool collage

Age range
Seven upwards.

Group size
Large groups with individuals making separate items.

What you need
Copies of photocopiable page 117, scrap materials (such as fabric, paper, string, buttons, beads, milk bottle tops), adhesive, sugar paper, pictures of rock pools and seaweed.

What to do
Discuss with the children the sorts of shells, animals and seaweeds that are found in rock pools and ask them to make a collage. Some will be able to draw shapes free-hand on to fabric and paper before cutting them out, but others will be better using templates or paper patterns. Templates and paper patterns can be made simply by drawing the required shape on paper and cutting it out.

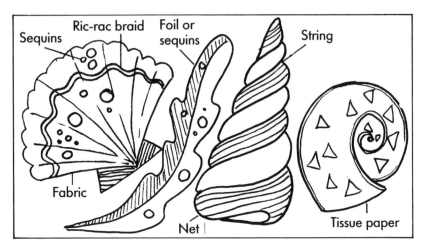

Use stiff paper for templates, and thin paper for patterns. Patterns should be pinned in place before cutting round them. Sample patterns are given on photocopiable page 117.

Let the children decorate the basic shapes using string, buttons, scraps of fabric or whatever scrap materials are available. Remind the children to cut out the basic shape first, then to stick the smaller objects on top of it. When the adhesive is dry, ask the children to cut round the shells and put them on one side until it is time to assemble the group collage.

Using pictures for reference, encourage the children to cut out shapes to represent seaweed, rocks, sea anemones and so on.

When all the separate items are completed, let the children assemble and arrange them on the background paper. They can move them around until they are satisfied with the picture, then stick them in place. Allow all the adhesive to dry completely before moving the collage, as heavy items may slide off.

A printed fruit bowl

Age range
Seven upwards.

Group size
Individuals or pairs.

What you need
A bowl, fruit, paper, pencils, corrugated card, paint, brushes, scissors.

What to do
Fill the bowl with a variety of fruit. Ask the children to make simple outline drawings of the fruit and the bowl. When these are complete, ask them to draw the outlines of the bowl and fruit on corrugated card. These shapes should then be cut out.

Paint can then be applied to the shapes using a brush. More than one colour can be applied at a time provided that gaps are left between colours to prevent smudging. Encourage the children to make test prints on scrap paper, before working on the final picture.

Easter eggs

Age range
Seven upwards (with adult help).

Group size
Large groups, with individuals making separate eggs.

What you need
Paper, white spirit and oil paint for the marbling, large sheets of paper or thin card for the background, adhesive, coloured paper, scraps of foil, scraps of gift wrapping paper, copies of photocopiable pages 118 and 119.

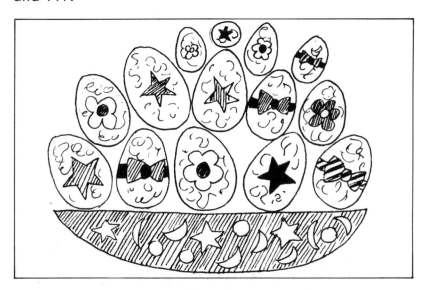

What to do
Marble the paper as described on page 37.

When the paper is completely dry, let each child cut out an Easter egg shape using the templates given on photocopiable pages 118 and 119. Ask the children to decorate the egg shapes by sticking on scraps of foil and paper in different colours.

Divide the class up into groups and ask a few members of each group to cut out a dish shape from plain coloured paper and decorate it using paper scraps. Let the children stick their dish shape on to the background paper or card, then encourage each group to arrange the egg shapes on the paper so that they appear to be in the dish. When the children are satisfied with their arrangements, let them stick them in place.

A painted landscape

Age range
Nine upwards.

Group size
Individuals.

What you need
Viewers (pieces of thin card with a rectangular hole cut out), copies of photocopiable page 120, paper, pencils, paint, brushes, pictures of landscape paintings.

What to do
Ask the children to look through their viewers at a landscape (this could be a view through a window). A template for a viewer is given on photocopiable page 120. Explain that the viewers can be moved around to frame different parts of the landscape, and so make it easier to decide which will make the most dramatic picture (see Figure 1).

When the children have chosen a view, ask them to make a sketch of it to show how it is divided into areas of grass, sky, fields and so on. Next, let them add

Figure 1

features such as trees, buildings and animals (see Figure 2). All this should be done using a faint pencil line.

When the 'skeleton' is in place, let the children use paint to fill in background colour and details. It often helps to apply a wash of a colour appropriate to the area being worked on, and then to modify it with smaller patches of colour on top. Show the children some landscape paintings by famous artists to see how they tackled similar problems.

Figure 2

A favourite toy

Age range
Ten upwards.

Group size
Individuals.

What you need
Toys (brought by the children), pencils, paper, pencil crayons, pastels or crayons.

What to do
Begin by looking at various toys and ask the class which basic shapes they comprise (see Figure 1). Then ask the children to make plans or construction drawings, like those in Figure 1, for their own toys. When these are

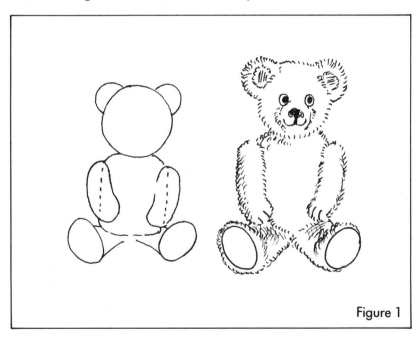

Figure 1

complete, shapes can be drawn more accurately, and features added. Depending on the toy, these could be ears, eyes or noses, or windows, doors or wheels. The preliminary construction drawings should be done using a faint pencil line (or pastel), so that alterations can be made without spoiling the picture.

Let the children add colours, taking care to mix them to achieve realistic shades. Shadows can be added over the base colour. Encourage the children to use purples, greys, browns and deeper shades of the main colour, as they will probably want to use black.

The background can be added either at the construction stage, or when the main drawing is complete. It could be realistic, that is, what actually surrounds the toy as it is being drawn, a memorised background, that is, what surrounds the toy at home, or totally imaginary, for example, a toy car could be pictured in a busy street.

Materials

Every activity in this chapter is based on the qualities and properties of the materials used. Natural objects, as well as scrap materials, are all put to good use and the materials suggested can all be found and stored easily.

The activities allow the children to experiment with a wide range of materials and techniques, for example, printing with small pieces of polystyrene. At the same time they will help children to develop an appreciation of colour, light and texture.

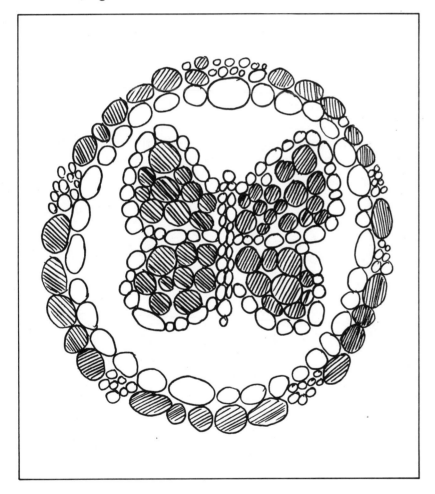

Pebble pictures

Age range
Five upwards.

Group size
Individuals or pairs.

What you need
Plenty of pebbles in a variety of sizes and colours, a large plastic tray with sand in it, paper, pencils.

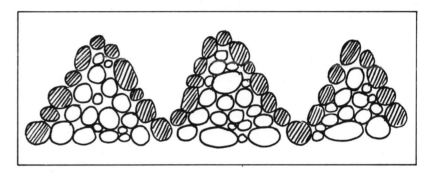

What to do
This activity is best done outdoors or in an area which can be easily swept in case of accidental spillages.

Ask the children to collect pebbles and bring them into school. Let them familiarise themselves with the pebbles by playing simple games such as rolling them on the ground. Encourage them to classify the pebbles in terms of shape, size and colour, then to use these classified groups to make patterns or possibly pictures in the sand tray.

Older children can make designs on paper, then translate them using stones. A worthwhile project would be to make a permanent pebble pattern outside in the school grounds (such as cobble stones or a mosaic).

Printing with packaging

Age range
Five upwards.

Group size
Individuals.

What you need
Polystyrene packing pieces in various shapes, paint, brushes, paper, fabric paints, pieces of fabric.

What to do
Show the children how to apply paint to the shapes and then print with them. Demonstrate how the shapes can be combined to make different patterns, then encourage the children to experiment.

Older children could use these shapes with fabric paints to decorate textiles or tee-shirts.

When the children have finished printing with them, the painted shapes can be used in a collage to make a relief pattern.

Bottle mobiles

Age range
Six upwards.

Group size
Individuals or pairs.

What you need
Green plastic drinks bottles, strong scissors, hole punch, thread or yarn, adhesive, scraps of coloured acetate film, foil.

What to do
As a class, look at the bottles and discuss their properties. Ask the children which of these properties are relevant to making mobiles. Lead the children to realise that the fact that the bottles are green and

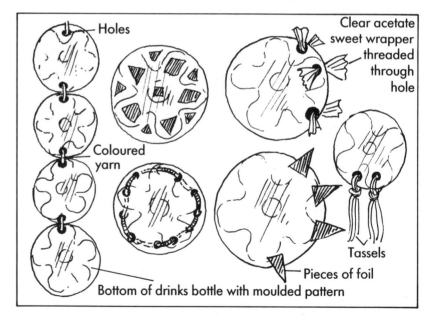

Holes

Clear acetate sweet wrapper threaded through hole

Coloured yarn

Tassels

Pieces of foil

Bottom of drinks bottle with moulded pattern

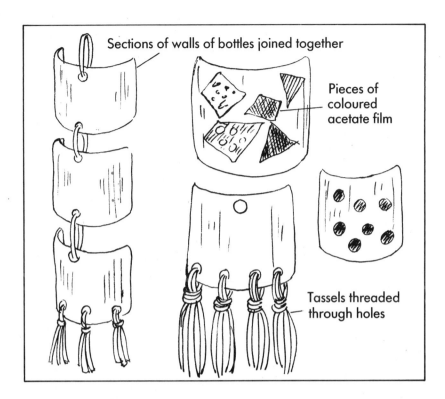

Sections of walls of bottles joined together

Pieces of coloured acetate film

Tassels threaded through holes

translucent is relevant, but the fact that they hold water is not.

Discuss the various ways in which the bottles could be cut up in order to make attractive mobiles. Examples of these are shown in the illustrations. Using a strong pair of scissors, cut the bottles up for the children in whichever ways they choose.

Encourage the children to experiment with decorating the bottle pieces. Suggest that they punch holes in them, either to join them together or purely as decoration, or attach pieces of coloured acetate film or foil.

When the children have decorated the bottle pieces, let them string the pieces together by threading yarn through the holes made by the punch. The mobiles will look most effective if hung near a source of light.

Decorative hangings

Age range
Six upwards.

Group size
Individuals or pairs.

What you need
A selection of nets (for example, an old string bag, bits of fishing net, fruit and vegetable nets), lengths of string, yarn and various types of thread, scraps of fabric, bodkins.

What to do
Discuss the materials with the children, and suggest ways in which yarn and fabric scraps might be knotted or threaded through the mesh of a net. Invite ideas from the children, too.

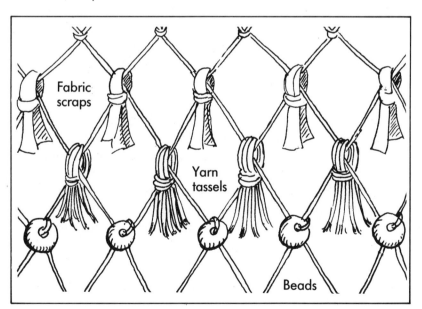

Fabric scraps

Yarn tassels

Beads

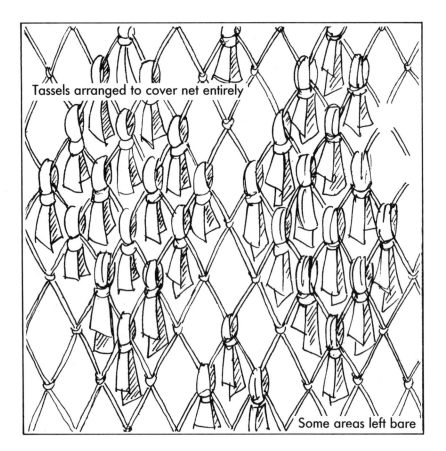

Tassels arranged to cover net entirely

Some areas left bare

Ask the children to experiment with some of the techniques discussed before actually making a hanging.

The children should consider colour combinations; contrasting colours could be placed next to each other, or colour might be used to make a simple pattern or motif. On a fine-meshed net, some areas could be left bare, with other areas entirely covered by knots or tassels. Bodkins are useful for working on fine-meshed nets.

When the children are confident with the various techniques, allow them to design and make their own wall hangings.

Cotton reel sculptures

Age range
Six upwards (with adult help).

Group size
Whole class working individually and in small groups.

What you need
Empty cotton reels, thin dowels or string, adhesive, shoe boxes, scissors, gift wrapping paper, fabric scraps, coloured thread and yarn, sequins, glitter.

What to do
As a class, look at and discuss the materials. Show the children how cotton reels can be threaded on to thin dowels or string, and how the reels can be rotated when they have been threaded. Discuss how the reels might be decorated with the various materials available. Point out that, since the reels can be rotated, any decoration should cover the entire surface of the reel.

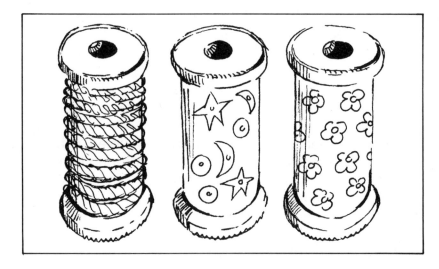

Allow the children each to decorate a reel. They could do this by:
- Winding round knitting yarn of different colours;
- Sticking on brightly coloured gift wrapping paper;
- Sticking on sequins and glitter.

Ask a few small groups of children to decorate shoe boxes, either by painting them or by sticking on decorative material. Let the children make a series of holes along the longer sides of the shoe boxes as shown in Figure 1 (adult help may be required here).

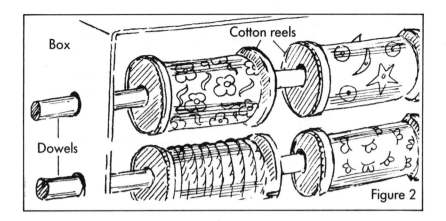

Figure 2

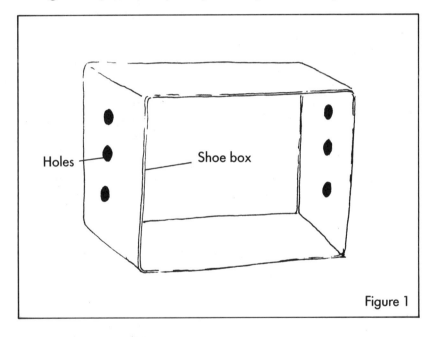

Holes

Shoe box

Figure 1

When the reels and the boxes are completed, ask the children how many cotton reels they think will fit on to a dowel suspended inside the shoe box. Discuss how the decorated cotton reels should be grouped together in the most attractive way. When the children have reached agreement about the arrangement, ask them to push a piece of dowel carefully through one of the holes into the box, thread cotton reels on to it, then push it out again through the hole on the other side of the box as in Figure 2. Repeat this with the rest of the dowels and cotton reels.

Making a screen

Age range
Six upwards.

Group size
Individual contributions to a joint effort.

What you need
A large quantity of polystyrene packing pieces, if possible in a variety of shapes, needles and thread, water-based paint, brushes, garden cane.

What to do
Let the children examine the packing pieces and look at the different shapes. Ask them to decide on a colour scheme and a sequence for threading the shapes (if they are not all the same).

Let the children paint the shapes, but remind them to paint both sides, letting the first side dry before painting the second.

When the shapes are dry, they can be threaded on to strong thread. Each individual thread can be tied to a horizontal garden cane and the cane can be secured against the top of a window.

The packing pieces can also be used to make attractive mobiles.

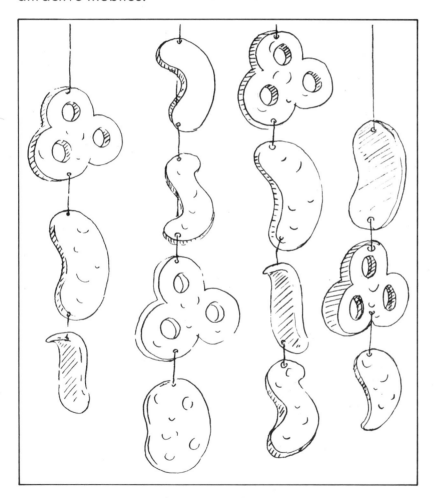

Bottle fish

Age range
Seven upwards.

Group size
Individuals or pairs.

What you need
Green or colourless plastic bottles, pictures of brightly coloured fish, paper, pencils, coloured acetate film, foil, adhesive, scraps of coloured paper and card, scissors.

What to do
Before the activity, cut the tops of the bottles, as shown in Figure 1.

Show the children pictures of brightly coloured or iridescent fish or, if possible, let them look at some real fish in a tank. Encourage the children to look at the various shapes of fins and tails, and look for colours and patterns in their scales. Let them record these patterns by making coloured sketches.

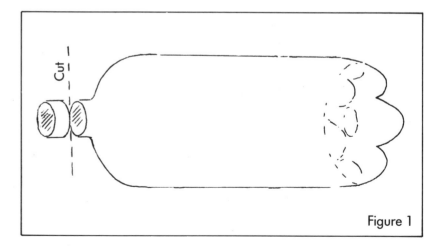

Figure 1

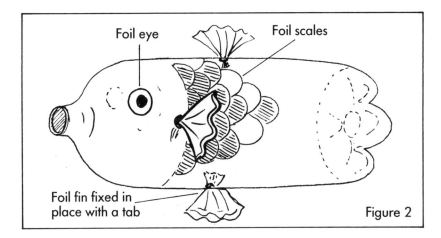

Foil eye

Foil scales

Foil fin fixed in place with a tab

Figure 2

Ask the children to make three-dimensional fish using the plastic bottles. Encourage them to use their sketches for reference and remind them that they will have to adapt them because of the limitations of the materials. Show them how to cut scales and eyes from foil paper and stick them to the bottle. Help them to make holes in the bottle and poke through fins and tails made of acetate film or foil. The fins and tails can be secured by folding tabs to insert through the holes.

Some ideas for bottle fish are given in Figures 2 and 3.

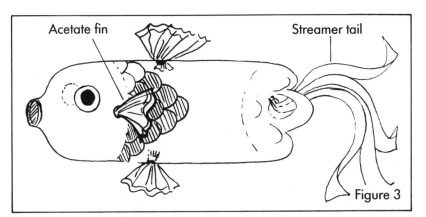

Acetate fin

Streamer tail

Figure 3

A woven hanging

Age range
Seven upwards.

Group size
Individuals or pairs.

What you need
Nets (for example, fruit or vegetable nets), fabric strips, bodkins or safety pins, drawing pins or adhesive tape, beads, felt scraps, scissors.

What to do
Show the children how to weave the fabric strips through the holes in the net using a bodkin or safety pin. Discuss how to make different patterns by changing the sequence of threading, and by changing direction (Figure 1).

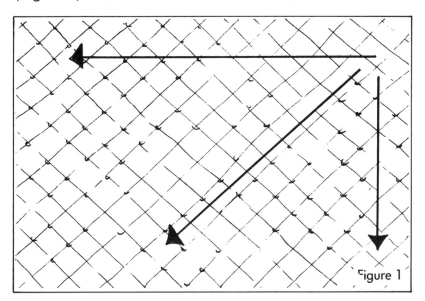

Figure 1

Discuss other ways of making patterns, for example, by changing the colour or texture of the fabrics.

Encourage the children to experiment with the materials before producing a finished hanging. They may find it easier to work with the net pinned to a board or taped top and bottom to a work surface.

Beads could be tied on to the net or threaded on to fabric strips for added interest (see page 25 on making beads). Another variation would be to stitch felt leaves or other motifs to the net.

Wristbands

Age range
Nine upwards.

Group size
Individuals.

What you need
Plastic drinks bottles, pictures of ethnic jewellery, scrap materials such as scraps of acetate film, paper, foil, fabric, string, polystyrene packing, scissors, adhesive, spreaders, hole punch.

What to do
Before the activity, prepare the drinks bottles by removing the necks and bases. Slit the remaining cylinders up one side, and cut them into sections around the circumference (Figure 1).

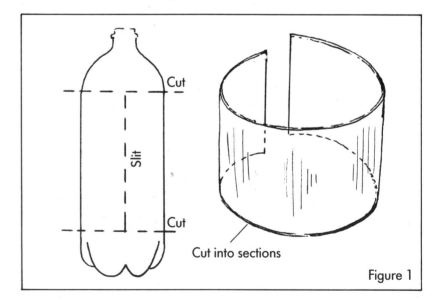

Cut

Cut

Slit

Cut into sections

Figure 1

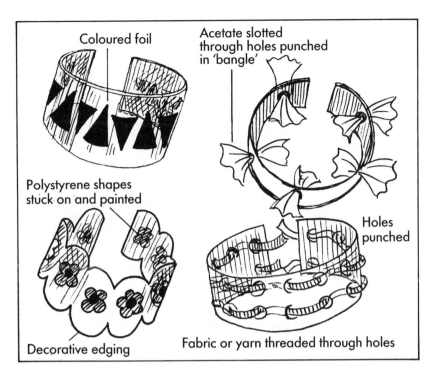

Coloured foil

Acetate slotted through holes punched in 'bangle'

Polystyrene shapes stuck on and painted

Holes punched

Decorative edging

Fabric or yarn threaded through holes

With the children, discuss the functions of arm bands and bracelets. Look at pictures of tribal and ethnic jewellery, and at items worn by ancient warriors in battle and for ceremonial purposes. Were these items used as personal adornment, purely as status symbols, or did they have a practical function too?

Consider the materials available, and discuss how they could be used to make wristbands. Then encourage the children to experiment before designing and making their prototypes.

Ways of using the materials listed above are shown in the illustrations. The scrap materials can be stuck to the outside of the bands or pushed through holes. Yarn or fabric can be threaded through a series of holes, while the edges of the bands can be scalloped, making sure there are no sharp points.

A fleecy wall-hanging

Age range
Nine upwards.

Group size
Individual contributions to a joint effort.

What you need
Roughly-spun fleece, dyes, wool yarn, card for looms, scissors, large piece of fabric for backing, bodkins, pictures of woven hangings.

What to do
First make cardboard looms as shown in Figure 1. If reasonably strong corrugated card is used, the children

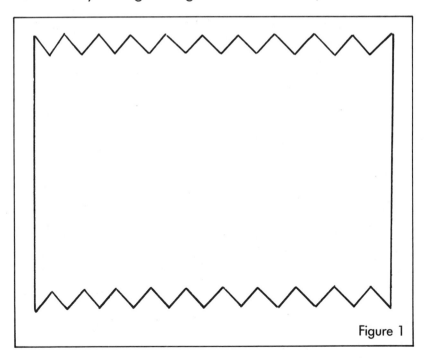

Figure 1

should be able to cut their own, but they will need help with any thicker card.

Show the children how to put the warp threads on to the looms (Figure 2).

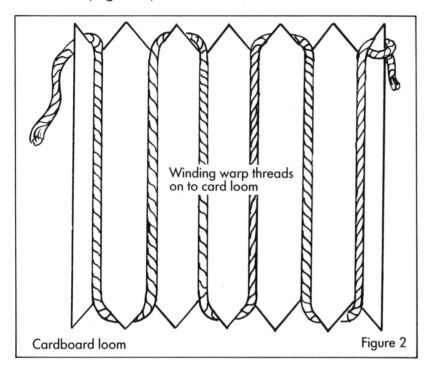

Winding warp threads on to card loom

Cardboard loom

Figure 2

If the spun fleece has not previously been dyed, dye it according to the manufacturer's instructions, using three or four colours if possible.

Show the children pictures of various types of woven hangings (and samples if possible), and discuss them. If the children want to weave or apply other materials to their work, encourage them to do so (see Figure 3). After the discussion session, let the children make up their individual samplers. When these are complete, pin or stitch them to the fabric backing to make one large hanging.

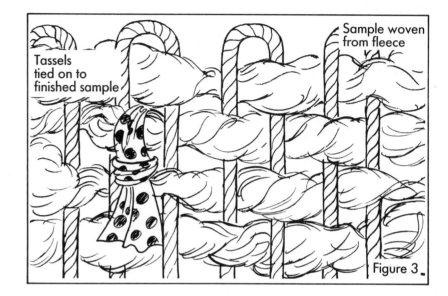

Tassels tied on to finished sample

Sample woven from fleece

Figure 3

Camouflage nets

Age range
Ten upwards.

Group size
Groups of four.

What you need
Thick yarn, roughly spun fleece or string, a dowel, thick knitting needles, scrap materials (such as fabric, paper, plastic), natural items (such as shells, seed pods, driftwood), paper, pencils.

What to do
Discuss the function of camouflage with the children, including both natural and man-made camouflage. Then consider the materials available to the class, and discuss how they might be used as camouflage, using a

net as their base. For example, on a beach, the most suitable materials to use would be string, to make a net, and shells, driftwood and other items that can be found at the seaside.

The scenes can be imaginary, or realistic, the only stipulation being that the materials used should be

Loop enough lengths of string over a dowel to give required width

Figure 1

suitable. Nets can either be knitted, or knotted as in Figures 1 and 2.

It is a good idea to make a work sheet, or ideas sheet

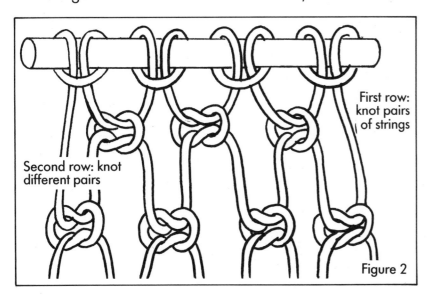

First row: knot pairs of strings

Second row: knot different pairs

Figure 2

for this type of project. This can be quite simple, but it will help children to clarify in their own minds what they have to do. Also, if they are working in groups, it can help you to assess the contributions made by each individual, so ensure that the sheets are made up individually. They should include sketches showing ideas, and notes about materials.

Natural objects

Many children are fascinated with natural objects. They offer them a variety of textures and colours and it is almost impossible to find two examples of the same object which are *exactly* the same.

The activities in this chapter require children to observe and record natural objects whch are easy to find. Drawing, modelling and making rubbings are among the activities included.

Apart from the variety of objects to hold, the beauty of working with natural objects is that many of them change over the seasons. Leaves, for example, can be drawn in the summer and again in the autumn. The children may be surprised at how their drawings differ.

Leaf drawings

Age range
Six upwards.

Group size
Individuals.

What you need
Leaves, wax crayons, sugar paper, pencils (optional).

What to do
With the children, study the shapes of various leaves. Look at the outline, and, if there is more than one section, notice how they are joined. Look at the veins and the patterns they make. Point out how they are connected in a regular manner, not randomly.

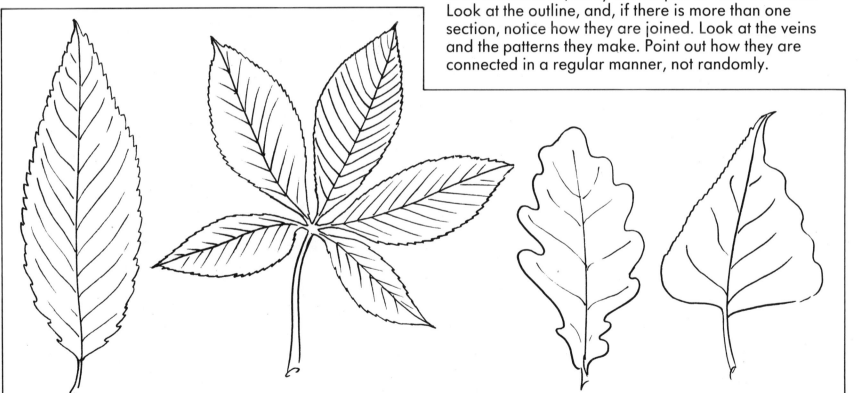

Next look at colour. Autumn leaves have bright colours, but some leaves are brightly coloured for the whole of their lifespan. Green leaves come in many different shades. Some leaves are variegated; some have spots or stripes.

When the children are ready to draw, invite them to make a rough plan of their leaf in pencil first (more experienced children can use crayon if they wish). Begin by drawing the main vein (Figure 1), then draw the outline round it (Figure 2). In the case of a compound leaf or one in which the main vein divides into three or more, draw all the main veins first (Figure 3), then add the appropriate outline (Figure 4).

With the skeleton in place, the children can work in crayon without having to worry about construction and can concentrate on colour and pattern.

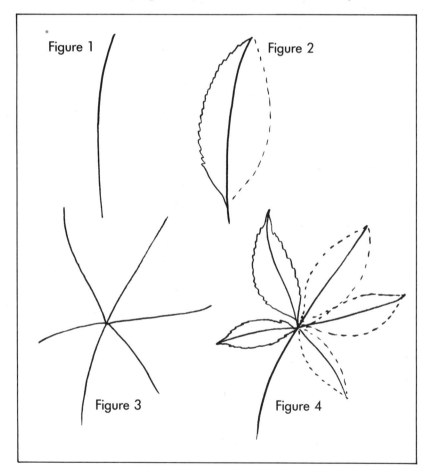

Figure 1   Figure 2

Figure 3   Figure 4

Collage of leaf rubbings

Age range
Six upwards.

Group size
Individuals for rubbings, individuals or groups for collage.

What you need
Leaves in a variety of shapes and sizes, paper (newsprint will do), wax crayons, scissors, background paper (preferably coloured or black), adhesive.

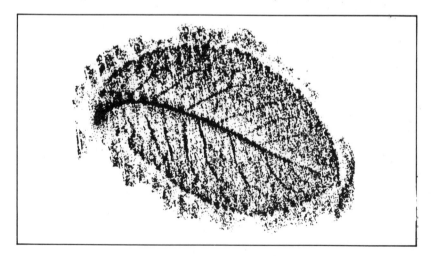

What to do

Ask the children each to choose a leaf and place it underneath a sheet of paper. Encourage them to rub a crayon gently, but firmly, over the paper where the leaf is hidden. The crayon will make stronger marks over the edges and veins of the leaf. Let the children repeat the process using different leaves and different colours. The rubbings can then be cut out and arranged on a sheet of black or dark-coloured paper. When the children are happy with the arrangement, let them stick their paper leaves in place.

As a variation, the rubbings can be carefully painted over with watercolour (the crayon will resist the paint). This will produce bi- or multi-coloured leaves with different textures.

Marbled jewellery

Age range
Five upwards.

Group size
Individuals.

What you need
Self-hardening clay in various colours, pebbles, varnish, jewellery findings, adhesive.

What to do
As a class, look at the pebbles and discuss the various colours in them and how some stones contain several colours. Encourage the children to look especially closely at stones with marbled patterns.

Let the children make marbled beads as described in 'Marbled beads' on page 20, flattening them slightly. When the beads are dry, allow the children to varnish them and mount them on jewellery findings. Encourage the children to compare their beads with the natural pebbles.

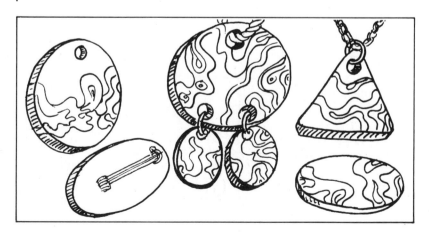

Painted jewellery

Age range
Seven upwards.

Group size
Individuals.

What you need
Self-hardening clay, assorted pebbles and stones, paint brushes, varnish, jewellery findings, adhesive.

What to do
With the children, discuss the colours and patterns on the stones.

Figure 1

Let the children make clay beads, as described on page 25, then flattening them slightly. Show them how they will stick them to the jewellery findings. When the beads are dry, let the children paint them with patterns and colours based on those they have studied on the stones and pebbles. Some suggestions are given in Figure 1.

Let the children mount their beads on jewellery findings, either singly or in multiples.

Follow-up
Let the children experiment with other shapes for their jewellery, such as triangles and ovals.

Feather designs

Age range
Seven upwards.

Group size
Individuals.

What you need
Feathers, paper, drawing tools (such as wax crayons, pastels, pencils, felt-tipped pens, pencil crayons).

What to do
With the class, look at a wide variety of feathers. Allow the children to hold the feathers to experience just how light they are. Have one or two extra feathers which can

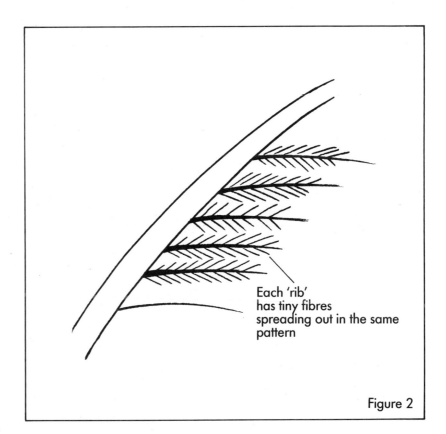

Each 'rib' has tiny fibres spreading out in the same pattern

Figure 2

be mistreated to demonstrate their strength. Look closely at the structure of feathers, and draw diagrams on the board to illustrate this.

Next, note the variety of colours and patterns in your selection. Many birds have feathers of more than one colour, and sometimes of more than one pattern too (for example pheasants, many types of duck and finches).

Now ask the children to make their own drawings. These should show the qualities discussed above, but in separate drawings as in Figures 1 to 3. For example, make separate sketches to show shape, structure, colour and pattern. Don't let the children cram all the information into one drawing.

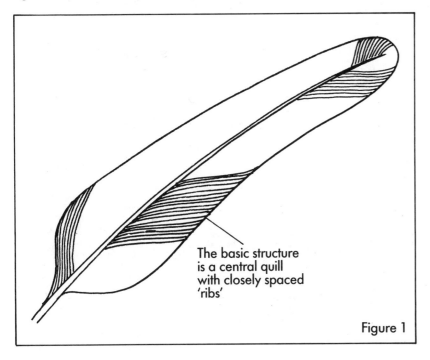

The basic structure is a central quill with closely spaced 'ribs'

Figure 1

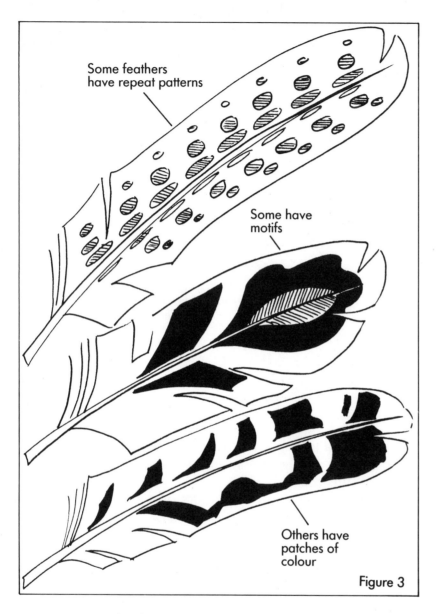

Some feathers have repeat patterns

Some have motifs

Others have patches of colour

Figure 3

Having made sketches, the children can develop designs from them by isolating motifs and combining them in various ways.

Shell designs

Age range
Seven upwards.

Group size
Individuals.

What you need
Shells, paper, drawing tools (such as wax and pencil crayons, felt-tipped pens, pencils, pastels).

What to do
As a class, look at different types of shells and discuss their characteristics: shape, colour, size, texture. Talk about the structure of the shells, and illustrate them on the chalkboard.

Figure 2

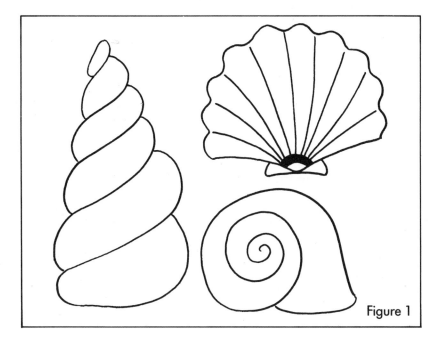

Figure 1

Then ask the children to make their own drawings of the shells. These do not need to be complex, in fact they can be very simple as in Figure 1. Let them try a variety of media such as pencils, charcoal and wax crayons if possible, then choose one to work with.

Let them go on to use these drawings to make shell-based designs. The shell drawings can be used in various ways: as single motifs; repeated to make a pattern; and combined with other motifs to make a complex design (Figure 2).

Display the finished designs in the classroom, and then keep them for future reference, as they can be used for embroidery or to decorate pottery and clothing, to name just a few examples.

Sunflower plaque

Age range
Seven upwards.

Group size
Individuals.

What you need
Sunflowers or daisies, flour, water, salt, paint, brushes, drawing materials, rolling pins, cutters, damp sponge, an oven, cooling rack.

What to do
With the class, look at sunflowers or any other daisy-like flower and discuss their various component parts. Encourage the children to make detailed sketches of the flowers.

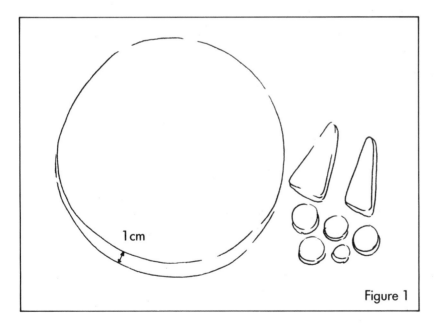

1cm

Figure 1

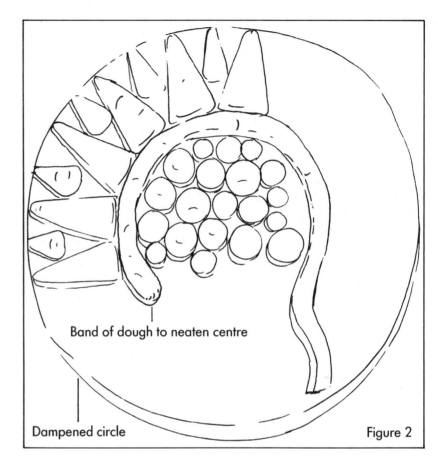

Band of dough to neaten centre

Dampened circle

Figure 2

Show them how to make a dough using one cup of salt to four cups of flour and one and a half cups of water. Ensure that they knead the dough well to make it pliable. Let the children roll out the dough to a thickness of about 1cm and cut out a large circle for the base of their plaques. Show them how to cut out triangles for the petals of their flowers and make small flattened balls of dough for the centre, as in Figure 1.

Get the children to dampen the large circle a small section at a time, and gently press a double row of petals and flattened balls into place, as in Figure 2.

Bake the dough plaques in an oven at gas mark 4 or 180°C for about one hour or until the dough has hardened. Allow the plaques to cool on a rack.

When the dough plaques have cooled, let the children paint them in colours that are as realistic as possible.

The dough plaques make attractive presents for the children to give on Mother's Day or they can be used to enhance a summer classroom display.

Felt jewellery

Age range
Eight upwards.

Group size
Individuals.

What you need
A variety of leaves, paper, pencils, felt (commercial or hand-made), needles and thread, wool yarn, fastenings (such as Velcro, safety pins, press studs).

What to do
As a class, discuss the variety of different leaf structures. Encourage the children to look at details such as veins and stems and make their own drawings. Let the children use these leaf shapes to design items of felt jewellery. Ask them to make sketches first to show how the motifs will be used. They could use a single motif, or combine two or more to make a more complex design.

Ask the children to cut out the same shape in different sizes, then place them one on top of another, or side by side.

They can then add details such as stalks and veins using embroidery stitches. Fastenings for the jewellery can be made using Velcro, plaited wool cords, safety pins or press studs.

String collage

Age range
Nine upwards.

Group size
Individuals or pairs.

What you need
Examples of woodgrain, drawing materials, sugar paper or card, string of various types, adhesive, spreaders.

What to do
Show the children examples of woodgrain and ask them to make rough sketches of the patterns they see.

Let them copy the pattern in pencil on to sugar paper

Leaf dish in clay

Age range
Nine upwards.

Group size
Individuals.

What you need
A variety of autumn leaves for reference, drawing materials, paper for templates, scissors, self-hardening clay, rolling pins, cutting tools, newspaper, damp sponge, paints, brushes.

What to do
Ask the children to look closely at the different leaves and make drawings of them, showing the basic outlines and the main veins.

Let them choose one of their drawings and make a large drawing of it as a template. Explain that a circle

or card, then show them how to apply adhesive to a small section of the paper and allow it to become slightly tacky before pressing string in to place, following the pencil lines. Encourage the children to work in pairs at this stage, one child arranging the string and the other applying pressure with the fingers until the string stays in place. Let them continue in this way until the whole sheet is filled.

Follow-up
To make a brighter collage, dye pieces of string made from natural fibres such as cotton or sisal, using dyes specially formulated for cotton. Make sure to follow the manufacturer's instructions carefully.

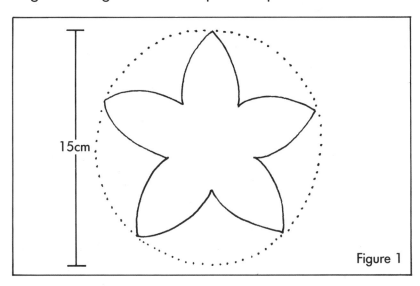

15cm

Figure 1

drawn round the template should measure at least 15cm across (Figure 1). Ask them to cut their templates out.

Let them roll out the clay and cut out a leaf shape by working round their templates. Show them how to draw veins on to the clay leaf by using a pointed tool.

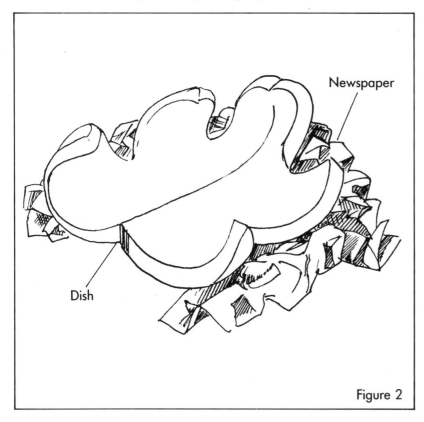

Figure 2

Ask the children to curl up the edges of their leaves gently so that a dish shape is formed. Explain that they should use crumpled newspaper to support the sides of the dish while it is drying, to prevent cracking (Figure 2).

When the dishes are dry, let the children carefully smooth the rough surfaces with a damp sponge and paint them in bright autumn colours.

Fruit embroidery

Age range
Ten upwards.

Group size
Individuals.

What you need
Pieces of fruit, knife, drawing materials, felt, a variety of coloured threads, needles with large eyes.

What to do
As a class, look at the various pieces of fruit and discuss their colours and shapes. Cut some of them open so that the children can see the patterns of the seeds inside. Encourage the children to work out a design for an

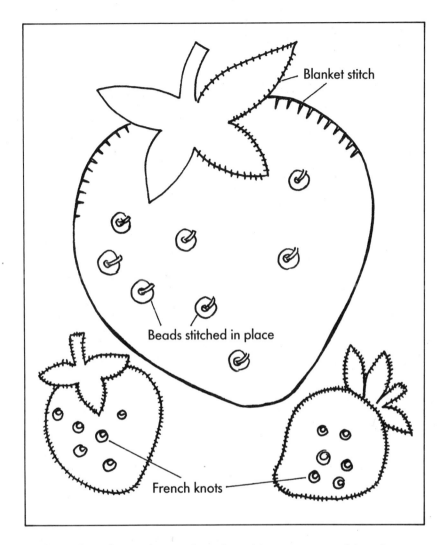

Blanket stitch

Beads stitched in place

French knots

could be added by using felt appliqué pieces or by sewing on beads.

Let the children use their original drawings as templates to cut out fruit shapes, then let them complete the embroidery.

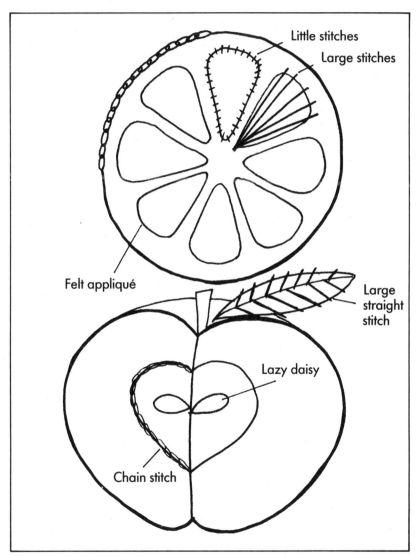

Little stitches

Large stitches

Felt appliqué

Large straight stitch

Lazy daisy

Chain stitch

embroidery based on what they have seen, taking into consideration colour, shape and texture.

Ask the children to consider what embroidery stitches they will use. For example, lazy daisy stitch can be used to suggest apple pips, French knots can suggest strawberry seeds, while chain stitch could be used to represent the bumpy texture of citrus fruits. Other details

Patterns

Most children enjoy creating patterns and will while away many an hour drawing patterns in the margins of books or other forbidden places.

The activities in this chapter suggest ways in which children can make patterns to great effect, without restricting their creativity.

A variety of materials has been included, for example, felt, wax crayons and tissue paper and the activities will help children to appreciate how patterns can be built up and how different components can be used together.

Crayon resist pattern

Age range
Five upwards.

Group size
Individuals.

What you need
Wax crayons, paper, paint, brushes.

What to do
Ask the children to use wax crayons in several different colours, and to draw a pattern made up of rows of shapes, for example, circles, triangles and zig-zags.

Explain that some shapes can be left as outlines, while others can be filled with a solid colour.

When the patterns are finished, let the children wash over them with watercolour paint to produce a two-textured design.

Follow-up
As an alternative, let the children use paper cut into a triangular shape or turn square paper at an angle to give a diamond shape.

Stained glass windows

Age range
Seven upwards.

Group size
Individuals.

What you need
Black paper, scissors, coloured tissue paper, adhesive, white paper or thin card.

What to do
Give each child a piece of black paper approximately 20cm square. Ask them to fold the paper into four and to cut out holes as though making a doyley (Figures 1 to 3). Remind them to leave sufficient black paper to stick

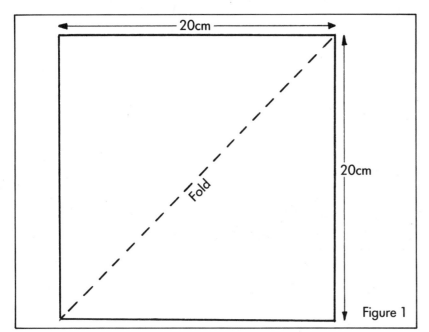

Figure 1

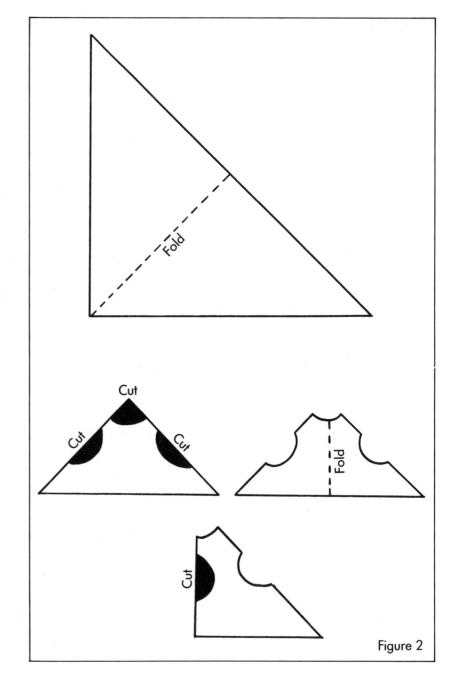

Figure 2

to the tissue paper. Allow them to fold the paper again and cut out some more shapes.

Let the children unfold the paper to see the patterns they have made. Show them how to cut out pieces of tissue paper that are slightly larger than the holes that have been cut in the black paper. Let them stick the tissue paper over the holes, but remind them that they should work carefully, using only small amounts of adhesive.

The finished patterns can be mounted on to black card to make one big stained glass window or stuck on to a real window so that the light can shine through.

Figure 3

Mosaic patterns

Age range
Seven upwards.

Group size
Individuals.

What you need
Gummed paper shapes or any small items obtainable in quantity (for example Smartie tube tops, milk bottle tops), adhesive, spreaders, background paper.

What to do
Let the children experiment by placing paper shapes in very simple patterns, such as concentric circles and squares. Encourage them to proceed to wave-like patterns, curves and spirals, and Paisley shapes. Their final design could be a combination of two or more different types of motif, or it could be a single motif repeated.

When the children are satisfied with their design, let them stick the units in place on the backing paper.

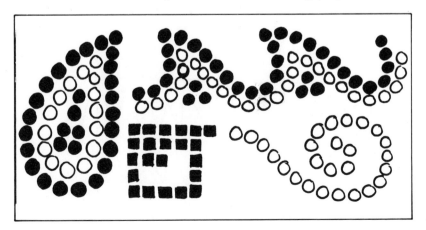

A triangle card

Age range
Eight upwards.

Group size
Individuals.

What you need
Pieces of cartridge paper, rulers, pencils, felt-tipped pens.

What to do
Give each child a piece of cartridge paper and ask them to fold it in half, then rule parallel lines across one of the sides, using the width of the ruler to ensure that the lines are the same width apart.

Figure 2

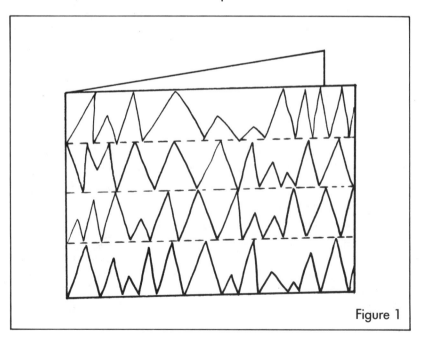

Figure 1

Ask the children to fill each row with triangles of varying heights and widths drawn freehand (Figure 1).

When the paper is filled, let them colour their triangles with felt-tipped pens, using block colours, patterns or a mixture of both (Figure 2). To combine this exercise with colour work, let the children try the following variations:
● A rainbow sequence, progressing through the colours of the spectrum and repeating the process until all the triangles are filled;
● Colour families using a mixture of as many warm colours as possible, such as reds, pinks, oranges and yellows, or alternatively as many cold colours as possible, such as blues, greens and blue-toned purples;
● Different shades of the same colour.

When the designs are finished, let the children write inside to make their own personal greetings cards.

A printed card

Age range
Eight upwards.

Group size
Individuals.

What you need
Books showing examples of folk art, drawing materials, paper, scissors, corrugated card, adhesive, paint, brushes.

What to do
As a class, look at examples of folk art and discuss how often very simple repeated motifs are used to great effect. Decide on a theme together, for example, 'birds in a tree' as shown here.

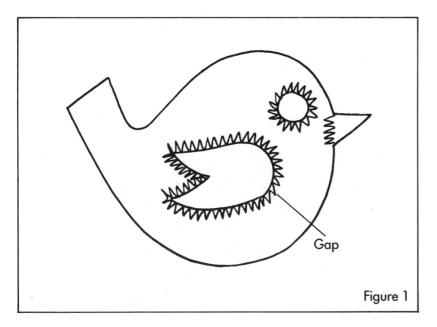

Gap

Figure 1

Ask the children to make sketches for the design, keeping outlines as simple as possible, then cut round the outlines and stick them on to corrugated card. When the adhesive is dry, let them cut out the shapes to make printing blocks.

Encourage the children to apply paint to the blocks and explain to them that more than one colour can be used, provided that sufficient space is left between the colours to prevent the paint running (Figure 1).

Let the children use the block to print on to the paper, and show them how to press the back of the block gently but firmly to secure a clear impression.

Using triangles

Age range
Nine upwards.

Group size
Individuals.

What you need
Copies of photocopiable pages 121 and 122, paper, pencils, felt-tipped pens or pencil crayons, gummed paper and scissors.

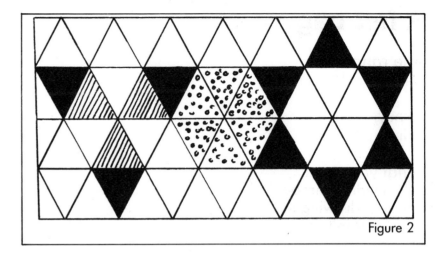

Figure 2

What to do
Distribute copies of photocopiable pages 121 and 122 and let the children cut out the templates. Allow the children to draw round the templates to make stars, hexagons and larger triangles, as illustrated in Figures 1 and 2.

Ask the children to use colour to break up the shapes in different ways. After they have experimented in this way, encourage them to make a repeat pattern, as shown in the illustrations.

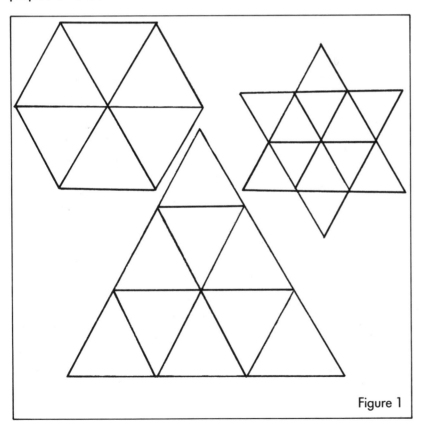

Figure 1

A felt bag

Age range
Ten upwards.

Group size
Individuals.

What you need
Felt, needles, thread, beads, wool for shoulder strap or hangers, drawing materials, copies of photocopiable page 123, felt scraps, adhesive, spreaders.

What to do
If possible, show the children some ethnic bags and pouches. Tell them that they can make a similar one for themselves from felt and that they should work out a design or pattern to be applied to the felt. They ought to bear in mind the materials to be used, and how much the bag will be used. For example, will the bag be used

every day, and in what circumstances? If the bag is to carry items to school regularly, embroidery stitches will need to be small so that they don't catch on anything, while applied details, such as felt or fabric scraps, would be better stitched rather than stuck in place.

Many ethnic patterns use geometric motifs, and these would be ideal for this piece of work (see photocopiable page 123 for idea for geometric patterns). Let the children consider different colours too.

When the bag has been designed on paper, let the children apply their designs to the felt. Then let them make up the bag by folding the felt in half and stitching along both sides using running stitch or using a sewing machine.

A strap for the bag can be made by plaiting wool, and securing the ends of the plait with knots (see illustration). For added interest, beads can be threaded on to the strands of wool as it is plaited, or threaded on to tiny plaits which can then be attached to the bag with a few stitches.

Geometric shapes

There is a wide range of activities in this chapter: from making jewellery out of small pieces of felt and cardboard to making a panel with patterned tiles. But they all have in common designs which are based around geometric shapes.

As they carry out these activities, children will develop an understanding of geometric shapes, for example, which shapes look most effective together, and they will learn to use lines, both straight and curved, and colour to their best effect. The activities include the use of clay, papier mâché and templates and the children will therefore gain valuable experience with a variety of tools, materials and techniques.

Sponge printing

Age range
Five to six years.

Group size
Individuals.

What you need
Sponge printers in various geometric shapes (see Tessellations 2, page 39), paint in margarine tubs, paper, newspaper.

What to do
Before the activity, make some sponge printers for the children as described in Tessellations 2, page 39.

Show the children how to dip their printers into the paint and print with them. Let them experiment with printing in a variety of shapes and colours, but make sure they blot their printers thoroughly on newspaper before using a different colour.

Encourage them to develop their printed shapes by drawing on details to make pictures of animals, people, houses, etc.

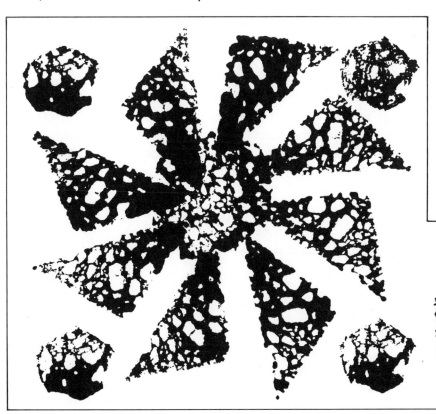

Over-printing with sponge

Age range
Six to seven years.

Group size
Individuals.

What you need
Sponge printers (see Tessellations 2, page 39), paint in margarine tubs, paper, newspaper.

What to do
Before the activity, make sets of sponge printers as described in Tessellations 2, page 39, so that the children have two each of the same shape, one large and one small.

Show the children how to use them by dipping them into the margarine tubs of paint and blotting them on newspaper before using a different colour.

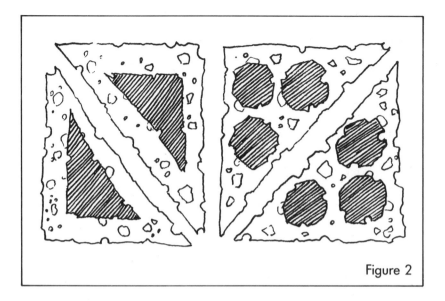

Figure 2

Ask them to print a pattern using the large printer, as in Figure 1, using colours which are light in tone such as yellows or pastel shades. When the paint is dry, ask them to over-print the individual shapes in darker colours using the small printers (Figure 2). Encourage them to choose colours which will contrast well with the original colours.

Figure 1

Geometric jewellery

Age range
Six upwards.

Group size
Individuals.

What you need
Felt, knitting yarn, needles and thread, adhesive, scissors, drawing materials, beads, sequins, buttons.

What to do

Let the children sketch ideas for jewellery using geometric shapes, or, if preferred, they can experiment directly with felt shapes. Have some geometric felt shapes ready cut for young children, but let older ones cut their own. Encourage them to try out different combinations, such as laying them side by side, one on top of the other, or overlapping. Beads, sequins or buttons can be used to decorate the shapes.

When the designs are ready, the children stitch the pieces in place. Stitching can be decorative as well as functional, particularly if a variety of stitches is used. Younger children may be happier fixing the shapes with adhesive.

Chains for necklaces and bracelets can be made from plaited wool yarn, while safety pins, attached with a few stitches, can be used for brooches and badges.

Older children may prefer to make badges and wristbands rather than brooches and bracelets.

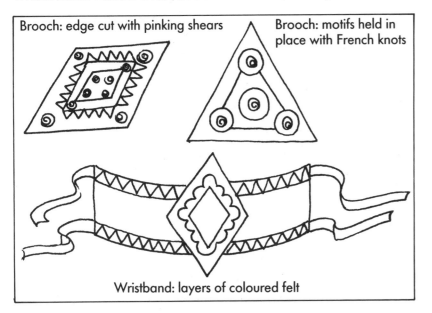

Brooch: edge cut with pinking shears

Brooch: motifs held in place with French knots

Wristband: layers of coloured felt

Cardboard jewellery

Age range
Seven upwards.

Group size
Individuals.

What you need
Drawing materials, gold and silver card, metallic yarn, adhesive, tape, coloured foil, sequins, scissors, safety pins, a leather hole punch.

What to do
Help the children to draw ideas for jewellery based on geometric designs.

Let them select one or two designs and make them up in card. When the children have cut out the shapes, holes can be punched in the card with a leather punch on the smallest hole. Metallic yarn or thread can be threaded through the holes to join the shapes.

For necklaces, yarn can be plaited to serve as a chain. Safety pins can be used for brooches; fix them to the back of the brooch with sticky tape.

Encourage the children to decorate individual shapes with sequins or coloured foil.

Geometric relief

Age range
Eight upwards.

Group size
Pairs or fours.

What you need
Corrugated card, pencils, copies of photocopiable page 124, scissors, paint, brushes, adhesive.

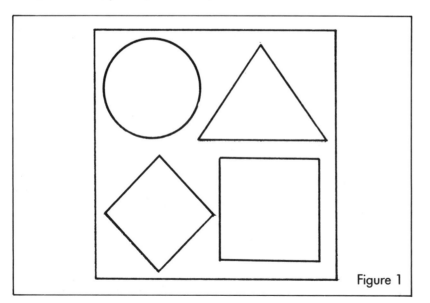

Figure 1

What to do
Give each pair or group a copy of page 124 to work from. Let them cut out varying numbers of each shape from corrugated card, for example, four squares, three triangles, one circle.

Ask the groups to place one of each shape in a grid arrangement on the corrugated card base; these can then be stuck in position (Figure 1). Then let the children stick, for example, all the other squares on top of the first square, and all the rest of the diamonds on top of the first diamond. As there are varying numbers of each

Figure 2

shape, the heights of each pile will differ (Figure 2).

When the adhesive is dry, let the children paint the reliefs. Ask the groups to do this in different ways; for example, one group could paint its relief in white only; another, in black only. Other variations include painting each shape a different colour; painting the shapes in patterns and their backgrounds in contrasting colours.

When the practical work is complete, put all the cards together, and discuss the effects of painting them in different ways. The all-white one, for example, will show more shadows, and so the effect of the relief will be

more obvious. The all-black one will appear flatter because the shadows will not show much. Patterned examples may appear flat, depending on the colours and patterns used.

Cardboard box sculpture

Age range
Eight upwards.

Group size
Pairs.

What you need
An assortment of cardboard boxes and tubes, a stapler, PVA adhesive, paint, brushes, newspaper and paste if required.

What to do
Give boxes and tubes to the children and let them fix them together using staples and adhesive to make a free-standing model. If they wish to make a stronger

model, they can coat it with papier-mâché.

When the model is complete, ask the children to paint it in one or more colours or give each shaped box its own pattern or colour.

The finished sculpture can stand on a surface or be suspended.

Dyed string collage

Age range
Nine upwards.

Group size
Pairs.

What you need
Various types of string made from natural fibres such as sisal or cotton, cold-water dyes in three colours, corrugated card, adhesive, pencils.

What to do
With the children's help, dye the string before it is needed, as it will need time to take the dye, and plenty of time to dry out. Be sure to follow the manufacturer's instructions carefully, otherwise results may be disappointing.

Between dyeing the string and making the collage, let the children work out a pattern using geometric shapes or simple curves. Some examples are given in the illustrations.

Ask the children to draw their designs on a piece of corrugated card using pencil or felt-tipped pen. When they are happy with the design, they can start to stick the string on to the card.

Adhesive should be applied to one section at a time and allowed to dry slightly before pressing the string into it. Ask one child in each pair to apply fingertip pressure until the string stays in place on its own. If both children each want to make a collage, they should finish one first before starting the other.

Hanging sculpture

Age range
Nine upwards.

Group size
Individuals or pairs.

What you need
Clay, rolling pin, batons or dowels, clay modelling tools, cutters or templates, paint, string.

What to do
Invite the children to roll out the clay with a rolling pin between batons or dowels (see page 33). They should then cut out a large triangle which will form the hanger for their sculptures. Next, ask them to cut out various geometric shapes in different sizes. Every shape must be pierced with a pointed tool. The hanger will need two holes, one at either end of its long side, plus enough holes along the other two sides for suspending all the small shapes (Figure 1).

Allow all the shapes to dry thoroughly, turning them daily to keep warping to a minimum. When the shapes

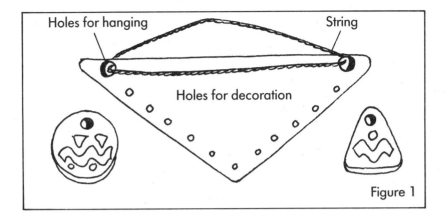

Holes for hanging

String

Holes for decoration

Figure 1

are dry, let the children paint them with bright colours, creating patterns if they wish.

Show the children how to loop string through the top two holes of the hanger, and attach all the small shapes to the hanger using string. Encourage children to work in pairs at this stage, as the hanger has to be balanced by adjusting the length of the strings holding the small shapes.

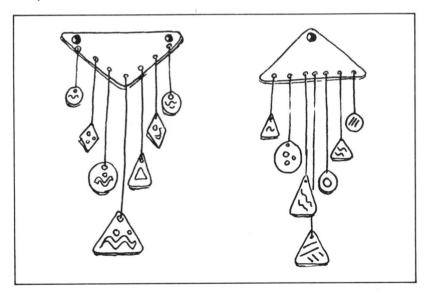

Papier-mâché cone

Age range
Ten upwards.

Group size
Individuals or pairs.

What you need
Newspaper, paste, thin card, a stapler, scissors, paint, scraps of foil and other decorative papers, cardboard tubes, wire.

What to do
Show the children how to make a cone from thin card stapled in place (Figure 1). Let them cover the cone with layers of pasted newspaper strips (Figure 2). Explain how it is imperative not to use too much paste as the cone will collapse under the weight.

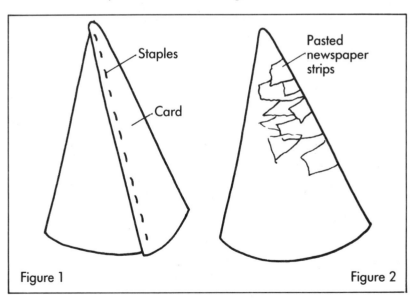

Staples

Card

Pasted newspaper strips

Figure 1

Figure 2

When sufficient layers have been built up, allow them to dry out completely, then ask the children to decorate the cones using paint and scraps of decorative papers in a geometric pattern.

The completed cone can be suspended on string, or can be supported with a stand made from wire or a cardboard tube as in Figures 3 and 4. The cones can be used as vessels for pencils or dried flower arrangements.

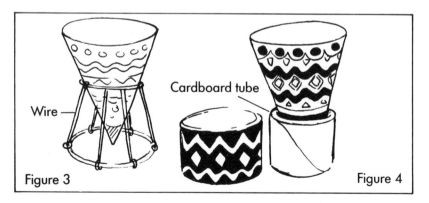

Figure 3

Wire

Cardboard tube

Figure 4

Tiled panels

Age range
Ten upwards.

Group size
Group project with separate pieces made by individuals.

What you need
Paper and pencils, clay, batons, rolling pins, cutting tools, modelling tools, templates or a tile cutter, sponge, kiln (optional), paint, brushes, hardboard, adhesive.

What to do
Begin by asking the children to work out designs for the tiles; this can be done individually or in small groups. Co-ordinate the work to avoid too many duplicate patterns.

Give some clay to each child and ask them to prepare it, roll it out and cut equal sized tiles from it (see page 34). The tiles should be 1 to 2cm thick. Explain that

everyone in the group should work with the same thickness, so that the tiles can be laid evenly on the panel.

The tiles can be decorated in clay relief (see page 34).

Allow the clay to dry, then smooth any rough surfaces with a damp sponge. If necessary, the clay can be fired. The tiles will look very attractive if they are painted. Mount the finished tiles on the hardboard, and display them.

Balloon mould vessels

Age range
Ten upwards.

Group size
Individuals, pairs or fours.

What you need
Balloons in assorted shapes and sizes, newspaper, paste, paint, adhesive, oddments of card, cardboard tubes.

What to do
Blow up the balloons and discuss with the children ways of combining the shapes. Remind the children that for the vessel to balance, the shape used on the bottom needs to be larger than the one on top of it.

Let the children choose which shape balloons they would like to use. Ask them to cover balloons with papier-mâché strips. Allow the shapes to dry out so that the balloon can be burst without the papier-mâché shape collapsing. Make sure that the balloons which will form the base of the vessels have a flat base. This can be done by pressing them gently on a work surface.

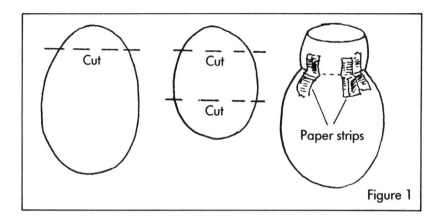

Figure 1

Allow the shapes to dry completely, then let the children cut holes where necessary, and join the shapes with strips of well-pasted paper (Figure 1).

Make sure that the vessels are completely dry before the children paint them with geometric patterns. These can be worked out on paper. Let them try different colour combinations, for example, neutral tones plus black, vivid primary colours, or a combination of hot pinks with yellow and turquoise.

Because of the time needed to dry out the papier-mâché, this project will take up more than one session.

Colour and light

The activities in this chapter have been chosen to help children to develop an awareness of colour and light per se, rather than being too concerned with how they are represented in pictures.

Children can observe the effects of light and colour by making simple moulded forms and sculptures from everyday items, by weaving different coloured fabrics together and by mixing colours together.

Colour sorting

Age range
Five to six years.

Group size
Whole class.

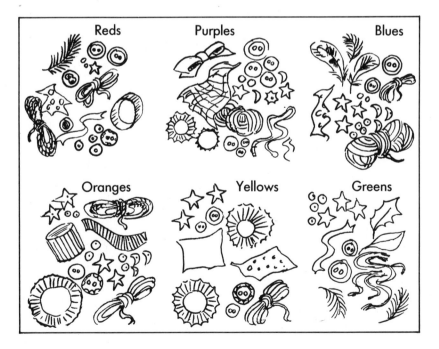

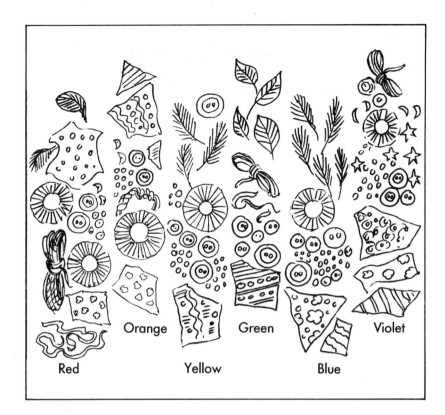

What you need
Scrap materials in as wide a range of colours as possible (for example, plastic, paper, fabric and knitting yarn), buttons, sequins, string, feathers, pressed autumn leaves, paper, adhesive.

What to do
As a class, look at the selection of materials available and sort them into groups of colours, ie groups of reds, groups of greens, etc. Some colours may be more difficult than others to classify. For example, should an orange/red colour go with the reds or with the oranges? Encourage discussion about such cases and reach an agreement.

Let the children try to arrange the different colours in a linear way like the arrangement of a new packet of coloured crayons.

When all the objects have been sorted to the group's satisfaction, ask the children to stick them on to a large sheet of paper, leaving room next to each object to label it, and display it for reference.

Rainbow picture

Age range
Six to seven years.

Group size
Individuals.

What you need
Photographs of rainbows, paints, brushes, wax crayons, felt-tipped pens, paper.

What to do
Discuss the colours of the rainbow and show the children photographs of rainbows if possible. Discuss how the colours in a rainbow are related to each other. Let them arrange crayons or felt-tipped pens in rainbow order.

Ask the children to make a picture of a rainbow in a landscape. Encourage them to think of different types of landscape so that the pictures have more individuality. For example, the landscape could be flat with trees silhouetted against the skyline; it could include a stretch of water in which the rainbow is reflected; or it could have hills, perhaps with sheep grazing beneath the rainbow.

Colour mixing

Age range
Seven upwards.

Group size
Individuals.

What you need
Sugar paper, pencils, rulers, paint, palettes, brushes.

What to do
Give each child a piece of sugar paper and ask them to divide their picture area into squares, using rulers as templates (see Figure 1).

Show them how to mix colours to produce a gradual change from one pure colour to the other (for example, begin with red and gradually add yellow to make it change through shades of red/orange to orange/red to orange and so on through to yellow).

One square on the paper should be painted with each additional shade. Older children should be expected to achieve more gradations than younger ones. The exercise can be done with just two colours or with more. It is also possible to use all the primaries to give a rainbow effect.

When the paintings are complete, compare them, looking at the quality of the painting, the number of gradations and the way the gradations have been arranged on the paper (see Figure 2).

If possible, show the children pictures of paintings by Paul Klee, who often used subtly changing colours painted in squares to build up a picture.

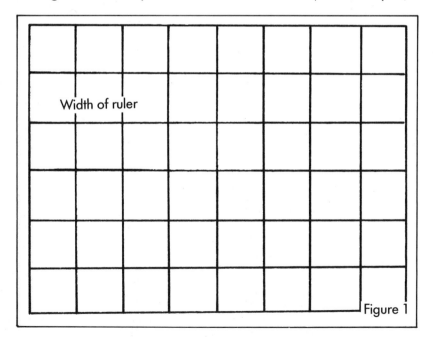

Width of ruler

Figure 1

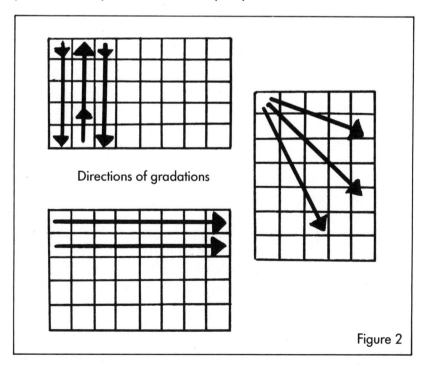

Directions of gradations

Figure 2

Paper collage

Age range
Seven upwards.

Group size
Individuals or pairs.

What you need
Magazines with plenty of colour pages, scissors, sugar paper, paste, spreaders.

What to do
Ask the children to tear up the colour pages from the magazines and sort them into piles of similar colours, so that they have a collection of different types of reds, yellows, blues, etc. When they have done this, discuss the colours. Some reds will contain blue, others yellow; some blues will contain yellow, others red. There will probably be some difference of opinion as to how some of the shades should be classified.

After discussion, ask the children to classify their colours further, sorting them into reds, blue/reds, yellow/reds, etc.

Ask them to choose one of the following groups:
• Red, orange, yellow;
• Yellow, green, blue;
• Blue, purple, red.

Let them make a collage using only colours from their chosen group. Encourage them to arrange the collage to show a gradual change across the picture from, for example, blue through green to yellow.

Woven panel

Age range
Eight upwards.

Group size
Whole class, with units made by individuals or pairs.

What you need
Wire coat-hangers, fabric cut or torn into strips 2cm wide, adhesive, scissors, needles and thread (optional).

What to do
Show the children how to pull the wire coat-hangers into a square shape, as in Figure 1.

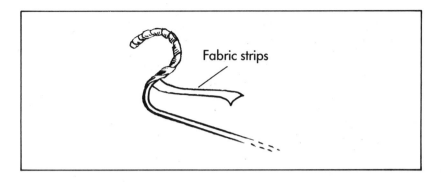

Fabric strips

Encourage the children to tie, stick or stitch more fabric strips to the frame and weave them in and out of each other and around the frame (Figure 2). Ask them to choose the colours carefully, perhaps using different shades of the same colour or complementary colours.

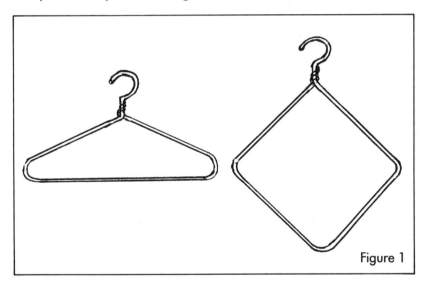

Figure 1

Give the children fabric strips to wind round the hangers so that the wire is completely hidden. Ask them to secure the ends of the fabric, either with adhesive or with stitching.

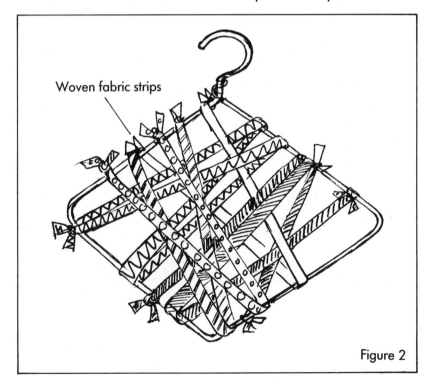

Woven fabric strips

Figure 2

When all the individual units are completed, ask the children to join them together with knotted fabric strips (Figure 3). Again, careful choice of colours should be encouraged when deciding where to place each section of the panel.

Make a hanging strap by plaiting fabric strips and display the panel against a wall.

An interesting and effective panel could be created by using pieces of fabric dyed by the children themselves, as the colours could then be chosen specifically for the panel.

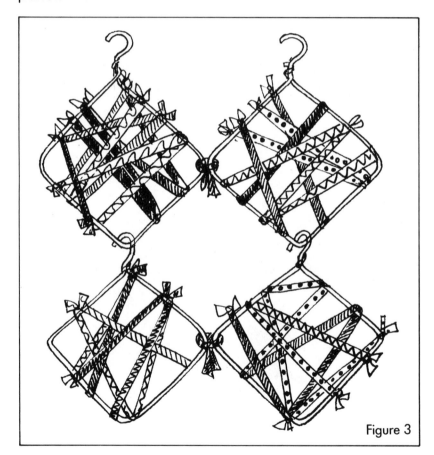

Figure 3

Stained glass roundels

Age range
Eight upwards.

Group size
Individuals or pairs.

What you need
PVA adhesive, margarine tubs, transparent polymer paint, tubs, mixing tools.

What to do
Pour PVA adhesive into mixing tubs, and ask the children to colour it with a small amount of paint. The more paint added, the stronger in colour and less transparent the end product will be, so the children will need to experiment. They should use a separate tool to mix each colour to ensure that the colours stay clean.

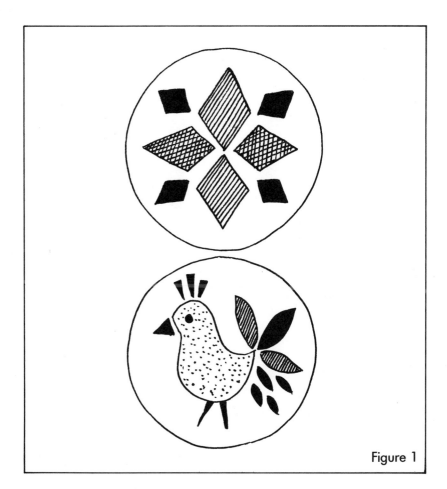

Figure 1

Pour a thin layer of plain PVA adhesive into each margarine tub, and add spots of colour to it. Let the children swirl the colours into a pattern or leave them as spots. Allow the adhesive to set completely. It will be transparent when it is ready, and can be peeled out of the tub. Let the children trim the edges and display their 'stained glass' against a window. If they wish, let them cut their 'stained glass' into different shapes (Figure 1). The shapes can also be made into mobiles and hung near a light source.

Experiments with colour

Age range
Eight upwards.

Group size
Whole class or small groups taken out from class (if you have assistance).

What you need
Translucent paper and acetate film in a variety of colours, patterned fabrics, dyes, strongly coloured objects, copies of photocopiable page 125.

What to do
Together, look at strongly coloured objects through the acetate film and translucent papers. Let the children

note and record the effect that each colour has on each object. This should be done in an orderly way so that the information gathered can be referred to and used at a later date.

Take the fabric samples, and cut each one into at least two pieces (you will need one piece as a control, and as many other pieces as you have dye colours).

Mix the dyes according to the manufacturer's instructions. With the children wearing protective clothing, let them dye the fabric samples, allowing plenty of time for the colour to develop (it is often better to leave them overnight).

When the process is complete, and the fabric dry and ironed, discuss the results with the class or group, comparing each dyed sample with its control. Record all the observations using photocopiable page 125, and display the results next to the samples of fabric. Discuss how this process relates to the original experiments with translucent paper and acetate film.

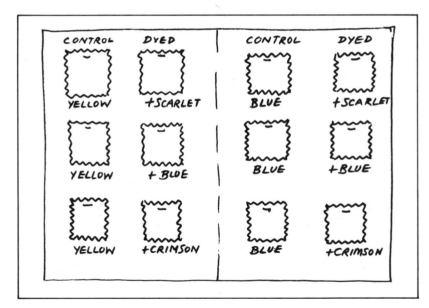

Night light holder

Age range
Ten upwards.

Group size
Individuals.

What you need
Clay, knitting needles of various sizes (or similar), sponge, paint, night lights, matches.

What to do
Invite the children to make a thumb pot (see page 23). It should be wide enough to hold a night light, and should be 7 to 10cm high. Tell the children to make it larger

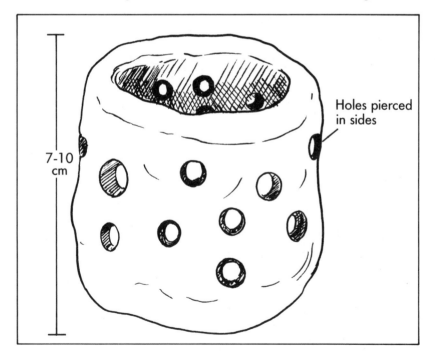

Holes pierced in sides

7-10 cm

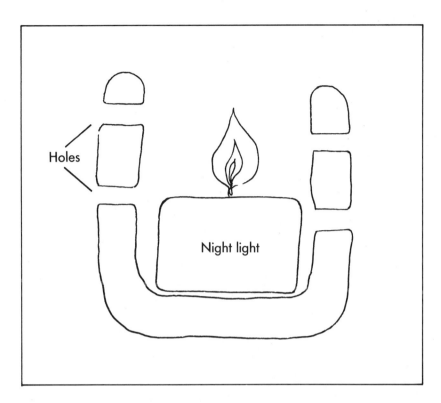

Holes

Night light

than the final pot is intended to be, because clay shrinks as it dries. Remind them to flatten the bottom of the pot by pressing it on a table top.

Using knitting needles, ask the children carefully to pierce the sides of the pot with several holes. These will allow light to shine through.

When the clay is dry, smooth away any rough edges using a damp sponge. Make sure that the sponge is damp and not wet, as excess moisture will cause the pot to collapse. Let the children paint their pots.

When the pots are completed, place a night light in each one and light it. If possible, enlist extra adult supervision at this stage and do not let the children touch the night lights. Darken the room and discuss the way in which the light forms patterns.

Card sculpture

Age range
Ten upwards.

Group size
Pairs.

What you need
An assortment of cardboard packaging (boxes, tubes), a stapler, adhesive, scissors, a sheet of card, paint, brushes.

What to do
Give the pairs of children boxes and tubes to arrange on a card backing to make an interesting design.

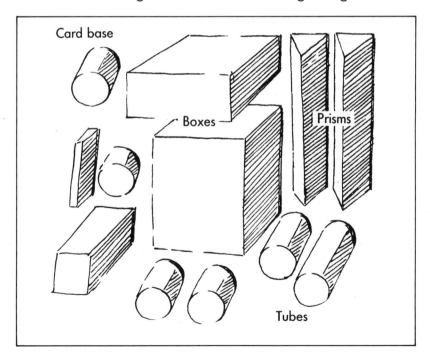

Card base

Boxes

Prisms

Tubes

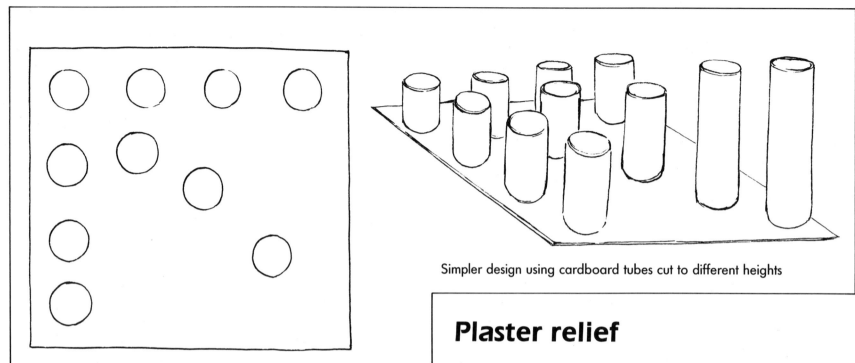

Simpler design using cardboard tubes cut to different heights

Encourage them to aim for variety in shape, size and height. When the children are satisfied with their arrangements they can secure the boxes on to the background using staples or adhesive.

When the adhesive is dry, let the children paint the reliefs. Ask each pair to paint their relief in a different way, for example, in a single colour, with a different colour for each box, or with patterns.

When the practical work is finished, look at the sculptures together and discuss what effects the various colours and patterns have. For example, a white-painted sculpture will probably show more obvious shadows than one painted with patterns.

Plaster relief

Age range
Ten upwards.

Group size
Individuals or pairs.

What you need
Drawing materials, Plasticine, modelling and cutting tools, dowels, release agent, plaster of Paris, paint brushes, board for base.

What to do
Although the children will be working individually or in pairs for the practical parts of this project, explain that the finished item is to be a group effort and that some group planning is necessary at the design stage.

As shown in the illustration, the finished panel will be made up of many individual pieces, each of which will be slightly different. Some pieces will be pierced, others will have projections, while others will have painted spots. Ask the class to decide how many of each type will be needed, how many colours to use and how the work will be divided among members of the class. This could be done either as a class with one large master plan made on the chalkboard, or each child or pair could make an individual plan and the class could decide which one to use.

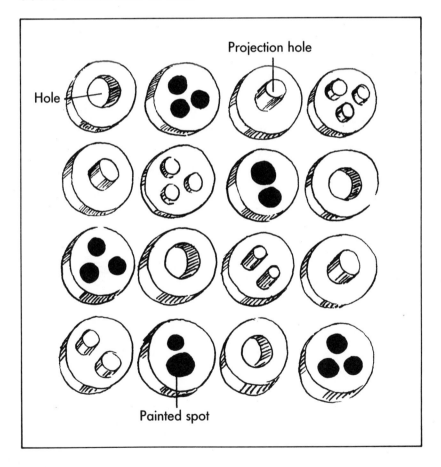

When the design has been chosen and the component parts allocated, let the children work individually or in pairs to make moulds from Plasticine. Ask the children to roll out the Plasticine to a depth of approximately 3cm and cut it to the agreed shape and size (Figure 1).

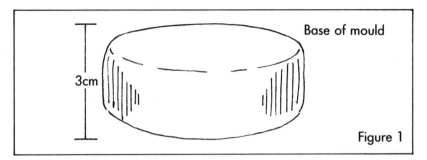

Figure 1

Let them make different relief patterns according to the chosen plan. To make projections, give the children dowels to press into the Plasticine to a depth of about 1cm. To make holes, let them press a dowel coated with a release agent into the Plasticine and leave it in position (Figure 2). Some moulds should be left plain.

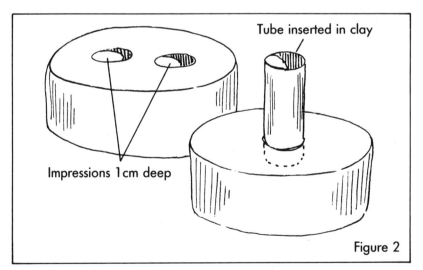

Figure 2

When this stage is completed, ask them to build walls around the edge of each mould to hold to plaster. This can be done by pressing a strip of Plasticine firmly around each mould, as in Figure 3.

Mix the plaster according to the manufacturer's instructions and pour it carefully into each child's mould and allow it to dry completely, preferably overnight.

When the plaster is dry, let the children remove the moulds and the dowels and paint the plaster pieces. When the paint is completely dry, ask the class to arrange the pieces on a base according to the original design and stick the pieces in place.

If possible, display the plaster relief near a source of light so that the children can observe how shadows affect the colours of the relief.

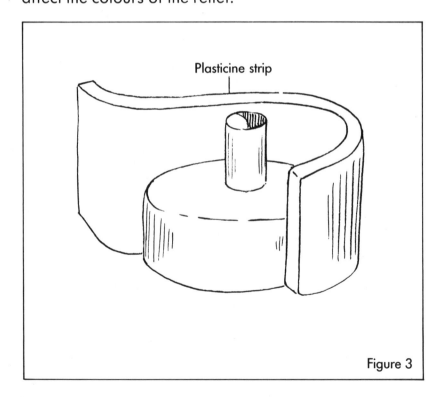

Plasticine strip

Figure 3

Make a mobile

Age range
Ten upwards.

Group size
Up to four.

What you need
Drawing materials, strong cardboard packaging (for example, card used for packing large electrical appliances), shears for cutting card, cardboard tubes, scraps of thinner card, adhesive, paper or fabric, paint.

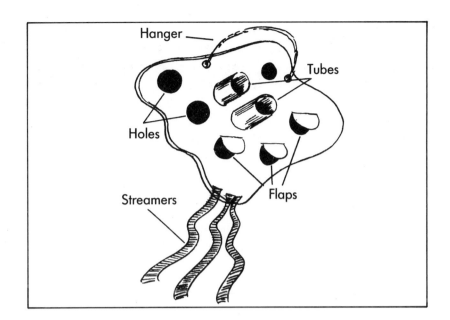

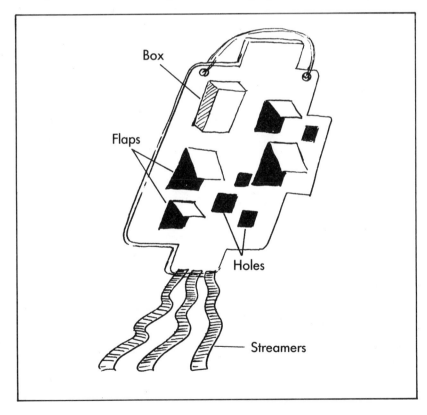

What to do
As a class, discuss ideas for creating a mobile. Encourage the children to make sketches of various arrangements of holes and projections, then ask them to work in small groups to create miniature mock-ups out of thin card. Ask each group to choose the design which is most satisfactory, bearing in mind that it is to be a hanging sculpture and so balance will be of prime importance.

Give the children the thick card and ask them to draw on the basic shape and cut it out with the shears. Some children will need adult help for this stage. Let them cut holes, add flaps and insert tubes where required. Adult help will probably be required for piercing the cardboard, so ask the children to occupy themselves by making coloured sketches while this is being done.

When the sculpture is complete, ask the children to paint it and add streamers made from fabric or paper. Some ideas for sculptures are given in the illustrations.

Glossary

For the non-specialist teacher, the following glossary of terms might be of use.

Collage
A picture or design made by sticking materials (for example, fabric, yarn, wood-shavings or paper) to a background.

Felting noils
Prepared short fleece of a quality unsuitable for spinning, but which felts easily. It is sometimes used for the filling layers of a felt item, rather than the surface, as it can have a rather rough appearance.

Findings
Fastenings, such as brooch backs and ear-ring clips, for jewellery.

Monoprint
Also known as monotype, this is a 'one-off' imprint of a design or picture drawn into or with paint. It is rather like butterflying, except that the paper is not folded to give a symmetrical design.

Relief
A design or picture with details which stand proud off the surface.

Sgraffito
A pattern made by scratching into a surface, eg wax crayon sgraffito. In pottery it can be used to decorate a surface.

Stencilling
A method of producing a repeat motif by applying paint through a stencil. A stencil is a motif or design cut from paper or, in industry, from metal or plastic. The cut out pieces are discarded and paint is applied through the holes.

Template
A pattern or shape to draw around.

Wash
Paint diluted and applied with a large brush over a large area. A wash is usually used as a background colour, but can also be used in resist techniques.

Wedging clay
The process of kneading and handling clay to make it uniformly pliable and to force out any air bubbles. It can be done either by kneading the clay as one would with bread dough, or by throwing the clay forcefully on to a suitable surface, such as an area of the floor covered with polythene. The clay is then sliced with a thin wire to check for air bubbles, then joined again by slamming the cut surfaces together forcefully to drive the air out from between them.

Wool tops
Top quality prepared fleece ready for spinning or felting. Often it will already have been dyed.

Reproducible material

Drawing basic shapes, see page 7

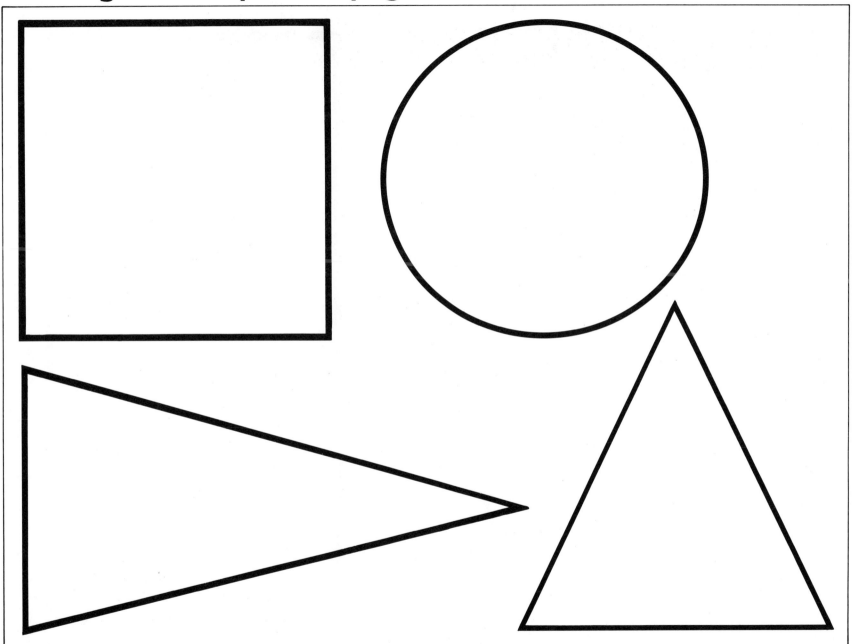

Drawing basic shapes, see page 7

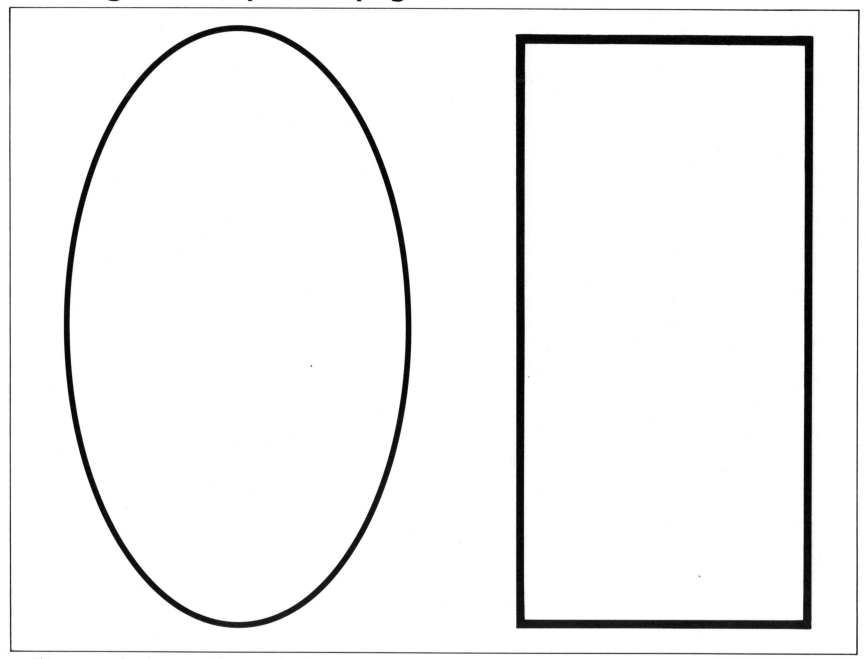

Giant food models, see page 16

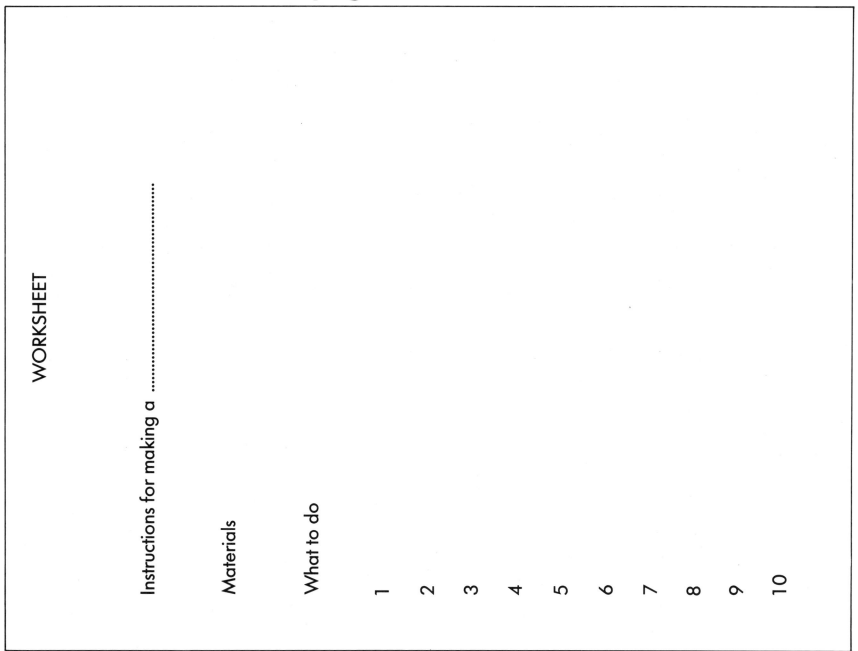

WORKSHEET

Instructions for making a ....

Materials

What to do

1

2

3

4

5

6

7

8

9

10

Printing shapes, see page 26

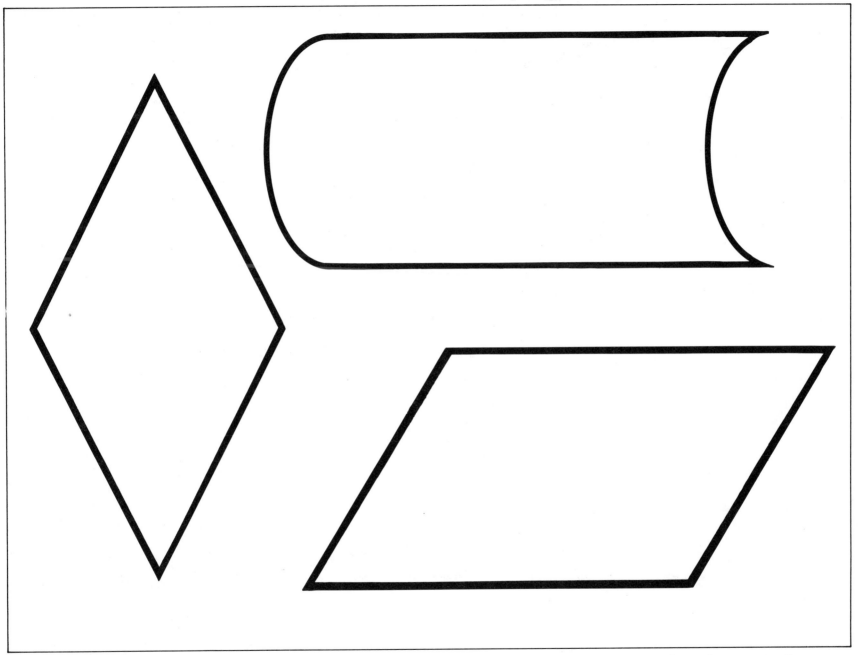

Tessellations 1 and Tessellations 2, see pages 38 and 39

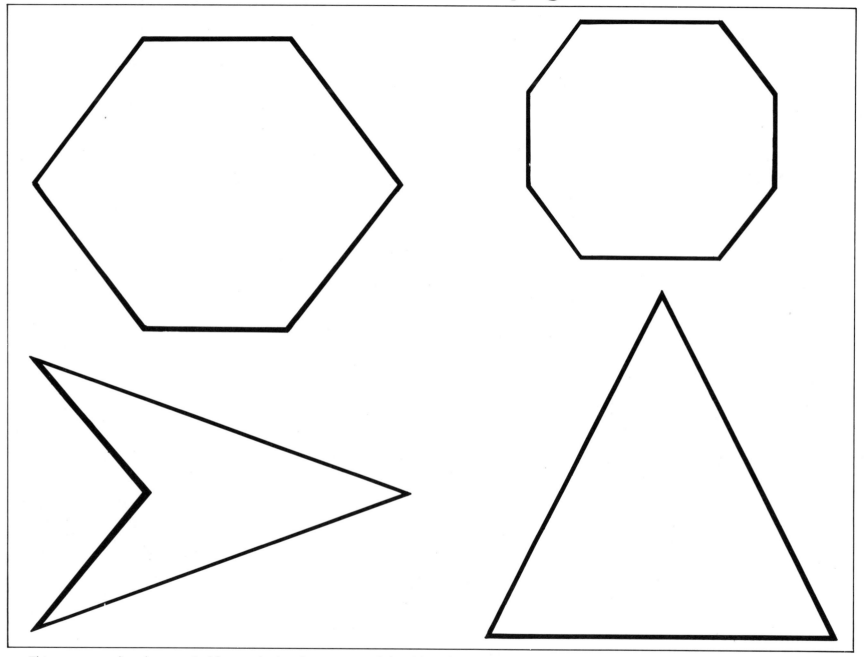

Rock pool collage, see page 46

Easter eggs, see page 47

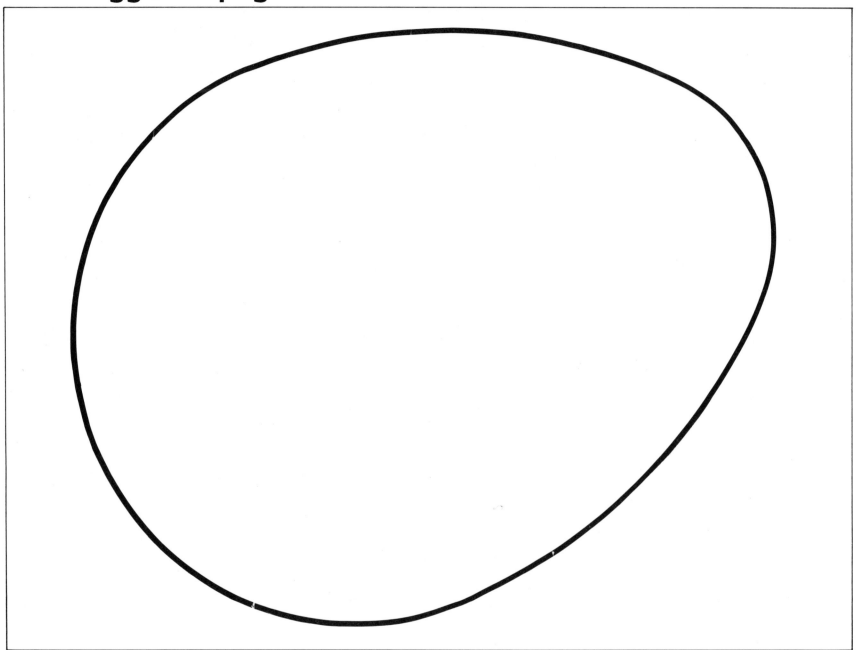

Easter eggs, see page 47

A painted landscape, see page 48

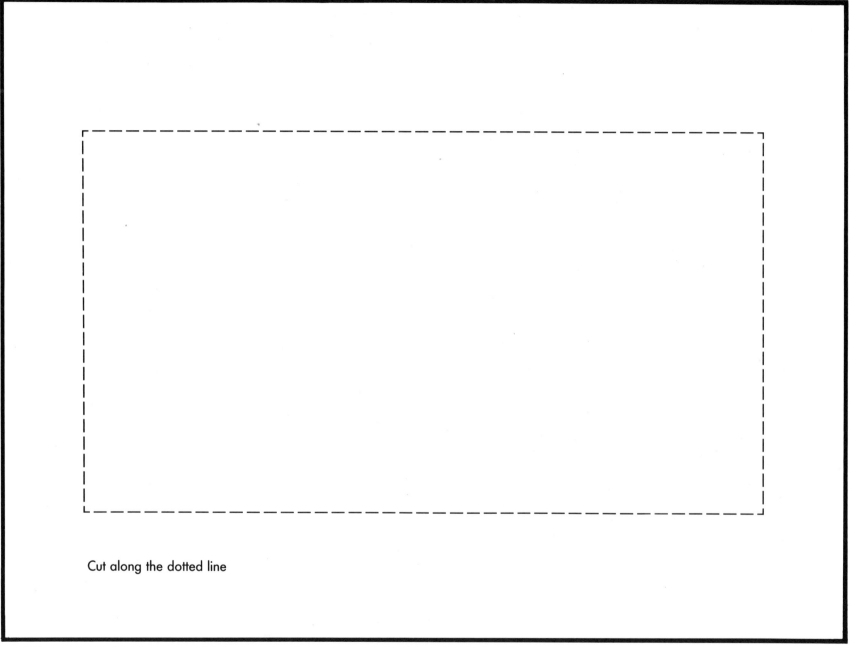

Cut along the dotted line

Using triangles, see page 82

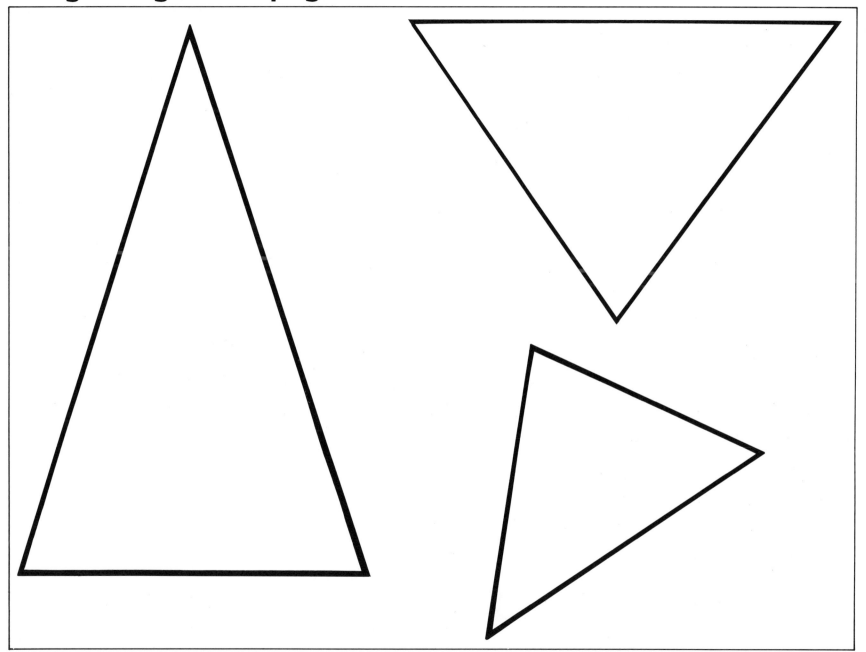

Using triangles, see page 82

A felt bag, see page 83

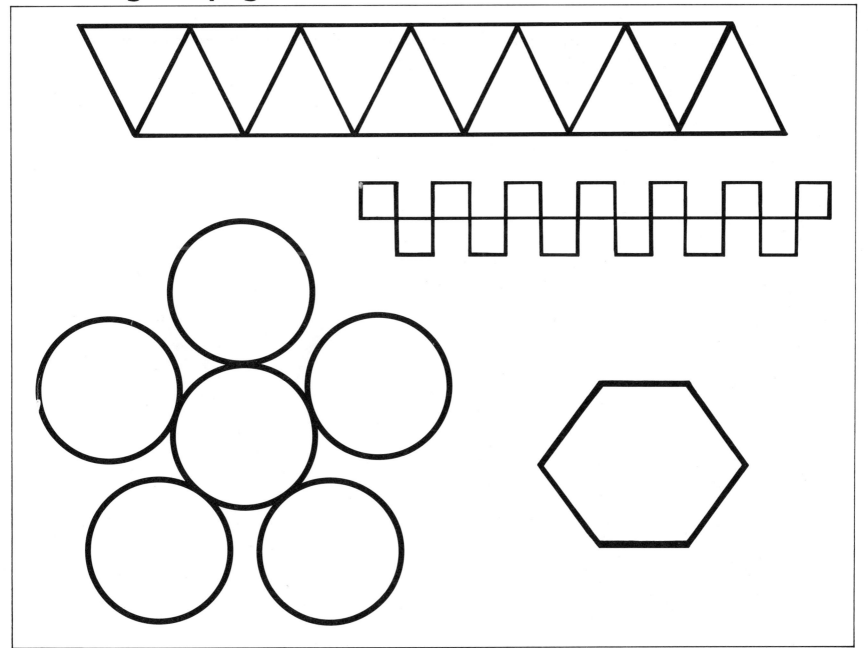

Geometric relief, see page 88

Experiments with colour, see page 101

RESULTS OF EXPERIMENTS WITH COLOUR

Name ....

Class ....

Type of fabric	Colour of fabric	Colour of dye	Result

Resources

The materials listed below are all suitable for use in schools, but care should be taken to follow the manufacturer's instructions at all times.

Adhesives

PVA
This is very versatile and can be used with most materials used in schools. Marvin Medium from Berol is particularly useful.

Multi-purpose adhesives
These are strong adhesives which can be used on glass, ceramics, metal and plastics. Bostik Multi-purpose is solvent-free.

Pastes
Pastes are useful for papier-mâché work and can easily be made from a mixture of flour and water. If using commercially-made paste, make sure that it is fungicide-free.

Paper and card adhesives
Gloy Gum and Bostik Paper Glue are safe for young children to handle and are solvent-free.

Mastic adhesives
Blu-Tack and Pritt are safe for children and can be re-used.

Paints
Berol pigment colours are water-based paints, formulated using pure pigments. They are intended for colour work.

Scholart Artform polymer paint is useful for papier-mâché work as it dries with an attractive sheen.
Scholart Multicrom is a transparent polymer colour and is ideal for monoprint and butterflying activities.

Pencils

Pencils are graded according to the softness of their lead. 'B' grades get progressively softer and 'H' grades get progressively harder.

Scrap materials

Encourage the children to be constantly on the lookout for useful scrap materials. Ask the children to grade it and sort it according to type and keep it in separate boxes.

Suppliers

E J Arnold & Son Ltd,
Parkside Lane,
Dewsbury Road,
Leeds LS11 5TD.

Berol Ltd,
Oldmedow Road,
King's Lynn,
Norfolk PE30 4JR.

Dryad,
PO Box 38,
Leicester LE1 9BU.

Galt Educational,
Brookfield Road,
Cheadle,
Cheshire SK8 2PN.

Nottingham Educational Supplies,
Ludlow Hill Road,
West Bridgford,
Nottingham NG2 6HD.

Osmiroid International Ltd,
Fareham Road,
Gosport,
Hampshire PO13 0AL.

Philip and Tacey Ltd,
North Way,
Andover,
Hampshire SP10 5BA.